Misplaced Date Digits Morgan Dollar Attribution Guide

by

Leroy C. Van Allen

&

Bill Van Note

Revised January 2009

1882 P VAM 24 Double 1 Base MPD

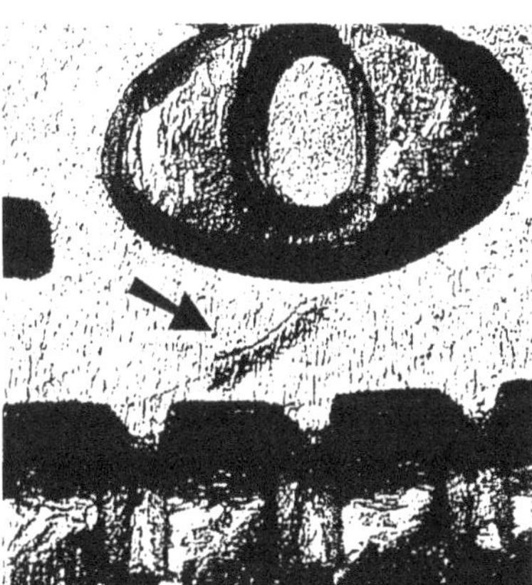

1882 CC VAM 2 1 Top Below 8

1903 S VAM 6 903 in Denticles

Hand Punching Die, 1970s

Published by

Rare Coin Investments (RCI)
P.O. Box C
Ironia, NJ 07845

Authors: Leroy C. Van Allen
Edited by: Michael S. Fey, Ph.D.

ISBN-13 number: 979-8-9919648-5-2

Printed in the United States

TABLE OF CONTENTS

LIST OF FIGURES

MISPLACED DATE DIGITS
MORGAN DOLLAR ATTRIBUTION GUIDE

INTRODUCTION

This is another update of the attribution guide to include additional newly reported varieties. The primary reason for this update is to include the recently listed 1882 P VAM 24 with ***interesting*** and **<u>different</u>** double partial left side of 1 base in the field below 18. Also added are the 1880 P VAM 51 with 8 in denticles, 1882 P VAM 23 with 8 in denticles, 1884 P VAM 17 with possible 4 in denticles, 1884 P VAM 18 with possible 8 in denticles, 1885 P VAM 28 with possible 8 in denticles, 1888 O VAM 33 with 8 in denticles, 1896 P VAM 26 with possible 9 in denticles, 1903 S VAM 6 with 903 in denticles and 1892 CC VAM 10A with clashed st.

Previous updates included new MPD varieties, expanded discussions, corrections to some listings plus some additional and improved photographs.

The misplaced dates are defined in Kevin Flynn's book *Morgan Dollar Overdates, Over Mintmarks, Misplaced Dates and Clashed E Reverses,* 1998, Archive Press, as "... occurs when the digits of the date are punched into the legend, devices, denticles, or any part of the field not normally associated with the general location of the date on the coin.... Misplaced dates are commonly referred to as MPDs."

These MPD die varieties are more accurately called **misplaced date digits**, since single to multiple digits are found beyond the usual location of the date. It is very rare that all four date digits are found misplaced. *Walter Breen's Complete Encyclopedia of U.S. and Colonial Coins*, Doubleday & F.C. I. Press, 1988, refers to this type of die variety as misplaced digits under the general category of blundered dies. However, the abbreviated term for **<u>m</u>**is**<u>p</u>**laced **<u>d</u>**ate of **MPD** is widely used at present. Perhaps **MPD** should more correctly be referred to as **<u>m</u>**is**<u>p</u>**laced **<u>d</u>**igits.

There are currently **56** known examples of misplaced date digits for the Morgan dollar and listed as die varieties in this report. The MPD examples have occurred on 33 different date/mint mark combinations from 1879 thru 1903 with **continuous** date examples from 1879 through 1892. They range from a single raised top of the curve of a date digit to the tops of **all four** date digits. Although most of the example MPDs for Morgan dollars have shown up in the denticle spaces near the rim below the date, there are also several **extreme** examples with the top of the 1 digit between the bottom of 8 and denticles, double bottom of 1 in field below 18, the bottom of a date digit occurring just below the Liberty head lower hair line and another with the bottom of a date digit on the Liberty head neck truncation. Undoubtedly, still more MPDs are waiting to be discovered.

MPDs on Morgan dollars were only recently first reported in 1990 with most being reported from 1998 and later. They are highly collectable die varieties with some being listed as Top 100 and Hot 50 varieties in the books, *The Top 100 Morgan Dollar Varieties: The VAM Keys* by Michael Fey and Jeff Oxman, 1996 and *SSDC Official Guide to the Hot 50 Morgan Dollar Varieties* by Jeff Oxman, 2000. There are even two **proof** Morgan dollars with MPDs in the denticles.

The intent of this Guide is to help **identify** the known Morgan dollar misplaced date digits varieties and to point out which ones are the most **desirable** to collect. A **Quick Attribution Summary Chart** is included for easy MPD variety identification that briefly describes what to look for, who reported them and when discovered. The possible reasons of how and why the MPDs occurred are examined along with a selection of the most visible and desirable Top 25 MPDs. A separate **listing** at the end of this Guide text provides detailed descriptions of each MPD variety. **Photographs** of each MPD and their associated die variety, if any, are provided at the end of this Guide.

The authors would like to see and examine any possible new MPDs that are not already listed. Leroy Van Allen can be contacted by mail at:

P.O. Box 196
Sidney, OH 45365
or by e-mail at: www.vams@woh.rr.com

HISTORICAL BACKGROUND

There were only **two** MPDs listed and shown but not recognized as MPDs in the VAM book, *Comprehensive Catalog & Encyclopedia of Morgan & Peace Dollars,* by Leroy C. Van Allen & A. George Mallis, DLRC Press 3rd ed.1992, & 4th ed.1998 reprint (VAM is taken from the first letters of **V**an **A**llen and **M**allis and a VAM number refers to a specific die variety). The first was the 1882 CC VAM 2 early die states reported by Charles Easterberg in November 1976 as a polishing mark below the left 8 that was pictured in the 1992 VAM book. It was later recognized by Jym Braun in August 2001 as the top of a 1 MPD. The second one was the 1886 P VAM 21 (formerly VAM 1B) which was reported by Bill Fivaz in January 1974 as a die gouge. But Bill Van Note recognized it as the bottom of an 8, an MPD, in November 1998. Generally, collectors hadn't been studying the Morgan dollar denticles where most of the MPDs are located as they were uninteresting uniform raised bars and spaces on coins. Most MPD digits in the denticle spaces aren't readily visible to the naked eye. It takes the use of a 7X or 10X hand glass to clearly see the digit tops in the denticle spaces in most cases. Collectors were not aware of the date digit tops in the denticles until someone took the time to study the denticles with a magnifying glass.

Walter Breen's 1988 *Complete Encyclopedia of U.S. and Colonial Coins book* had listed quite a few misplaced digit varieties as blundered dies from colonial coppers, large cents and Indian cents through other denominations up to twenty dollar gold coins. They included misplaced date digits all around the normal date position but mostly above or below the date. Examples of digits in the reeding or border were as early as an 1857 large cent with an 18 in the denticles. No listings of misplaced date digits were given for the Morgan dollar.

The **first** recognized misplaced date digit on the Morgan dollar was reported by Chris Pilliod in the October 3, 1990 issue of *Coin World.* It was an 1896 P VAM 19 variety with two raised curved bars of the top of an 8 in the denticle spaces below the 8 as shown in Figure 1. It wasn't until February and April 1997 that the next two MPDs were reported to the author by Bill Fivaz for the 1884 O VAMs 25 & 37 with examples of 188 and 18 in the denticles as shown in Figures 2 & 3.

The 1884 O VAM 37 shows a short vertical bar in the denticle space between the 18 which is the top right of the 1 and a faint raised curved bar well back in the denticle space below the first 8. It is a fairly weak MPD that takes a magnifying glass to see the raised tops of the 18.

The 1884 O VAM 25 is a bold MPD with a raised straight bar in the denticle space below the 1, a relatively thin raised curved bar below the first 8 and a raised curved bar with straight top below the second 8 and short curved bar in the adjacent left space. It is an unusual example MPD for the Morgan dollar with thin bars in the denticle spaces. (Another one being an 1890 O VAM 26 with 890 thin tops in the denticle spaces.) These bars appear to be thinner than the tops of the 8 digits even though the date digit sizes were reduced in 1884 for the Morgan dollar. A possible explanation is that the logotype punch of several date digits was tilted when struck into the denticles.

The other anomaly for the 1884 O VAM 25 MPD is the square top of the last MPD digit in the denticles. It has generated much speculation and suggestions as to the cause since it's discovery in 1997, but a satisfactory answer has not yet been put forth. Perhaps the square top was from an edge of a tilted logotype or even a letter punch that may have been sideways or upside down. As discussed in the later section, Possible Reasons For MPDs, any handy punch could have been used to create the marks in the denticles.

Bill Van Note became interested in MPD's after reviewing Walter Breen's *Complete Encyclopedia of U.S. and Colonial Coins* book. Van Note had also reviewed Larry Briggs's book on *Liberty Seated Quarter Dollars* that listed some dates with errant digit numbers on the working dies and another book that also included some errant date digits, *Liberty Seated Half Dollars* by Randy Wiley & Bill Bugert. Van Note was a member of the Indian Cent Club and began searching Indian cents for new MPD's and other types of varieties. The many new varieties he found are included in

Rick Snow's attribution guide on Indian cents.

Meanwhile, Bill Van Note had also studied misplaced date digits on the Morgan dollar since 1994. He provided the basis for the listing of 19 Morgan dollar MPDs in Kevin Flynn's book, *A Collector's Guide to Misplaced Date*, 1997 and the 37 Morgan dollar MPDs, including a number of questionable ones, listed in Flynn's 1998 book, *Morgan Dollar Overdates, Over Mintmarks, Misplaced Dates and Clashed E Reverses,* that had a chapter on Morgan MPDs. In January 1999, most of the MPDs listed in Flynn's 1998 book were examined by the author and 25 were selected as definite MPDs and included in a January 1999 VAM Supplement with descriptive listings and photographs. Thus, Bill Van Note was responsible for the emergence of the reporting of numerous Morgan dollar MPDs in Flynn's books and VAM book Supplements. He has reported, by far, **more** MPDs than anyone else and was responsible for almost half those currently listed in this Guide. He is truly the **pioneer** and **father** of the Morgan dollar MPDs!

This Guide lists and illustrates 56 MPD die varieties for the Morgan dollar. Four of these are **Top 100** varieties and are very popular including an 1885 S VAM 9 with 885 in denticle spaces, 1886 P VAM 21 with the bottom of an 8 below the designer's initial M, 1888 O VAM 9 with 18-8 in the denticle spaces and an 1896 P VAM 19 with 8 in the denticle spaces. Three of the MPDs are **Hot 50** varieties; the 1884 O VAM 25, 1888 P VAM 18 and 1900 P VAM 16. The 1884 O VAM 25 was listed as a **Hot 50** variety because of the entire date tops in the denticles but the other two were listed for other variety reasons, but the MPD of 8 and 900 respectively in the denticles was mentioned.

Figure 1 1896 P VAM 19 8 in Denticles

Figure 2 1884 O VAM 25 188 in Denticles

Figure 3 1884 O VAM 37 18 in Denticles

TYPES OF MORGAN DOLLAR MPDs

There are many different digit types and combinations of the 56 MPDs currently known for the Morgan dollar. Most are the **tops** of the date digits that show in the denticle spaces **below** the date. There are two that shows part of a digit in the field surrounding the date. The 1882 CC VAM 2 early die state with the top of a 1 between the bottom of the left 8 and the denticles. This is the **most visible** of all the Morgan dollar MPDs! The other MPD in the field between the date and denticles is the recently reported 1882 P VAM 24 with two partial bases of 1 tilted to the left below the 18. It is a very different MPD showing ghe two separate partial 1 bases. Two MPDs are known that show the **bottom** of the date digits above the date all the way up into the **lower hairline** of the Liberty head. Generally a 7X or 10X hand glass is needed to see most of the listed MPDs. This explains why MPDs were only fairly recently discovered on Morgan dollars.

All known examples of MPDs in the denticles occur just below the date digits in the field. But the MPD tops in the denticle spaces may not be directly below the corresponding digit in the field. They are frequently **shifted** to the **left** or **right** underneath the date in the field. Only the tops of the date digit punches of single or multiple digits would fit on the denticle space ridges between the recessed denticles on a working die. Any lower portion of a date digit in the denticle space (ridge on a die) would have resulted in the digit top being in the field below the raised date of a coin which has not been seen.

Another curious thing about the MPDs in the denticles is that the tops of the complete date are rarely found in an example MPD. The most frequently found MPD is that of a **single digit top**. Why this occurred is discussed later in the section, Possible Reasons For MPDs.

The known Morgan dollar MPDs are primarily found only in the denticle spaces and adjacent to the denticle space top. There are two MPDs in the lower hair line. Only two MPD are located in the field below the date and above the denticles, the very visible 1882 CC VAM 2 with top of 1 below the left 8 and 1882 P VAM 24 with double 1 base below 18 . There are many examples of slightly doubled date digits in the Morgan dollar series that are within the width of half a date digit. One would think that a punched date into a working die that was accidently placed beyond the normal position could happen at various places in the field. A discussion of why this didn't happen is presented in the later section, Possible Reasons For MPDs.

MPD Between Bottom of Date and Denticles

There are two examples of MPDs between the bottom of the date and denticles. The **most visible** of all the Morgan dollar MPDs, by far, is the top of a 1 digit between the bottom of the left 8 and denticles of the **1882 CC VAM 2 early die state** as shown in Figure 4. It is readily visible to the naked eye while all of the other Morgan dollar MPDs generally require the use of a hand magnifying glass to be seen.

This top of the 1 digit below the left 8 MPD was listed in October 2006 for the revised 1882 CC VAM 2 variety with a doubled 882. The curved bar between the denticles and bottom of the left 8 makes it the **outstanding** Morgan series MPDs and it's on a CC dollar!

This fabulous MPD has an interesting history. The 1882 CC VAM 2 with doubled 8 was reported back in June 1965 by George Mallis in a draft of a book *United States Silver Dollars Morgan Type* that was never published but became the basis for the 1966 revision of his 1964 book *List of Die Varieties of Morgan Head Silver Dollars.* The photo of VAM 2 in the 1971 and 1976 VAM books shows only the doubled right 8 with a raised die chip on the upper left loop, which is a good die marker for VAM 2.

On November 1976, Charles Easterberg reported an 1882 CC with extra metal around the reverse legend letters and polishing scratches on the obverse and reverse. It was listed as a new VAM 6 with doubled 82 and reverse letters with a description that included polishing marks below the first two right stars and heavy diagonal polishing mark below first 8. In March 1977, Oscar Simpson reported that the VAM 2 had doubling on 882 instead of just the right 8 with die chip on that 8 upper loop.

It was later determined in September1978 that the VAM 6 had a doubled 882 and was actually a die state of VAM 2. The 1992 VAM book VAM 2 photo of the Easterberg coin shows the complete date with the diagonal bar below the left 8 which was still thought to be a polishing mark at that time.

A letter from Jym Braun in August 2001 stated he had examined some 1882 CC and thought the diagonal bar was an MPD because the curve and length matched the top of the 1 digit. A note was made in the VAM book listing that the diagonal bar below the 8 could possibly be the top of a 1, but an early die state VAM 2 was needed for examination and photographing to revise the listing. It wasn't until October 2006 that a nice condition of an early strike VAM 2 was sent for examination. It was then confirmed that the diagonal bar below the left 8 had the same length and curvature with diagonal ends that matched the 1 top shape. Apparently the 1 was lightly punched into the die field at a slight tilt. Because of the diagonal bar's visible location and size, the Interest Factor was increased to I-5 for this early die state MPD. A later die state VAM 2B without the MPD and clashed n has had the diagonal bar and polishing lines removed by die polishing reducing it to I-2.

It should be noted that a VAM 2A die state with a faint partial clashed n at the neck with the 1 MPD was reported by Michael Ash in October 2006 and a VAM 2C with a die break at back of the Phrygian cap and counterclash doubled lip was reported by Laurence Galbraith in January 2006.

In summary, there was confusion in the 1970's with the listing of the 1882 CC VAM 2 early die states with polishing marks as a VAM 6. Charles Easterberg reported the polishing marks on the obverse in November 1976 and 25 years later Jym Braun pointed out in August 2001 that the diagonal mark below the left 8 looked like the top of a 1. In October 2006 the early die state 1882 CC VAM 2 was finally confirmed and listed as the most visible Morgan dollar MPD. Sometimes the most obvious things can be overlooked!

The other MPD with digits in the field between the date and denticles is the **amazing 1882 P VAM 24** with double partial 1 bases as shown in Figure 5. It was reported in May 2008 by Brian Raines and must be quite rare to have been undetected for all of these years. Perhaps this obverse die was further polished down early in it's life and the two 1 bases were removed. However, the die had already been severely polished with the 1 bases showing as evidenced by the gaps in the hair above the date. This die also shows a slightly doubled 882.

This interesting and different MPD has the left top horizontal and left vertical lines of the 1 base of two impressions separated by over a denticle width that matches the 1 digit left side. It is a unique MPD with the two partial impressions of the same 1 digit in the field below the date 18. The 1 punch had to have been tilted to the left and back to make an impression of only the left side of the 1 base.

MPDs in Denticles

The easiest identifiable MPDs are the raised curved bars that appear in the denticle spaces. These are the tops of a 2, 3, 8 or 9 date digits. No top of a 6 has yet been found. They can be located deep within the recesses of the denticle spaces, which can be a little hard to see, or anywhere along the length of the denticle space including projections slightly out in the field above the denticle space. Generally, it is desirable for the curved bars to be seen in **two adjacent denticle spaces** in order to confirm that the curve matches the top of the curved date digits. A bar or line in a single denticle space would be a fairly short segment of a curved date digit top and is difficult to positively match to a digit top. They could just be a die gouge or heavy polishing line unless a well defined bar shows.

An example MPD with the top of the 8 digit recessed into the denticles space is shown in Figure 6 for an 1881 S VAM 8. An 9 or 2 digit top at the outer edge of the denticle space is shown in Figure 7 for an 1892 CC VAM 10. An example of two digit tops in the denticle space is shown in Figure 8 for 1 and 8 tops of an 1884 S VAM 8. A nice example of three digit tops in the denticles is

Figure 4 1882 CC VAM 2 1 Top Below 8

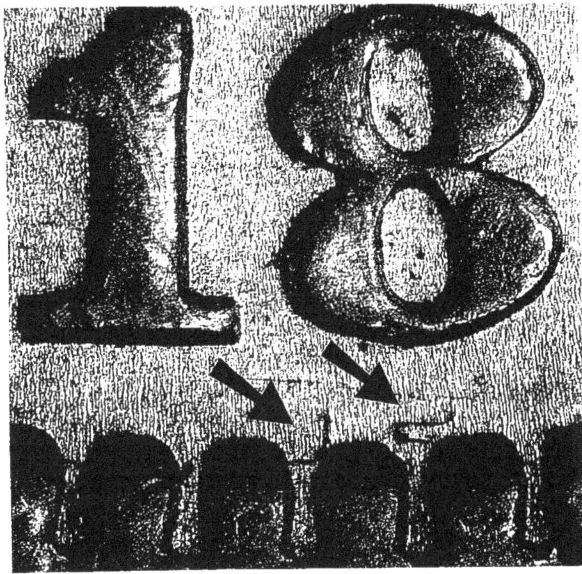

Figure 5 1882 P VAM 24 Double 1 Base MPD

Figure 6 1881 S VAM 53 Recessed 8 in Denticles

Figure 7 1892 CC VAM 10
High 9 or 2 in Denticles

Figure 9 1900 P VAM 16 900 in Denticles

Figure 8 1884 S VAM 8 18 in Denticles

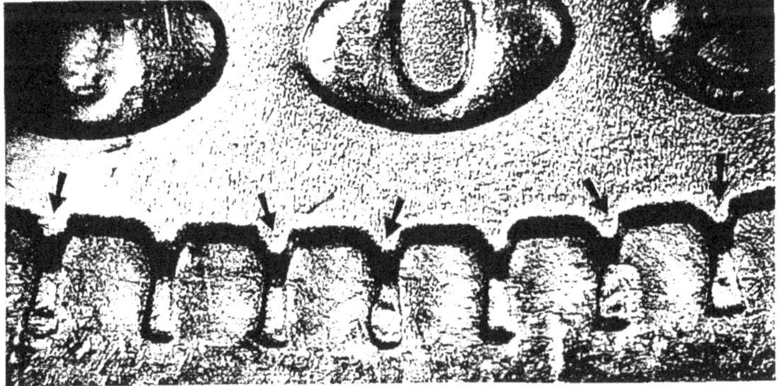

Figure 10 1883 O VAM 39 Four Digits in Denticles

shown in Figure 9 for the 1900 P VAM 16 with the 900 digit tops boldly in the denticle spaces.

There is one known case of all four date digit tops showing in the denticle spaces of the 1883 O VAM 39 as shown in Figure 10. The tops of the 883 are well recessed in the denticle spaces and the top of the 1 is faint.

A nice example of the top of a 1 is shown in Figure 11 for the 1888 O VAM 28 with square top bar in one denticle space and the slanted left top in the next left adjacent denticle space. The top of the 1 digit shows above the denticle in Figure 12 for the 1883 O VAM 40. There are even examples of the top of a 7 digit in two adjacent denticle spaces for the 1887 O VAM 27 shown in Figure 13. Thus, there are known examples of practically all date digits (Just missing only the 6.) in the denticle spaces.

There are two known examples of Morgan dollar **proof** dies with the top of a digit in the denticles, the 1888 VAM 25 and 1900 VAM 32. Figure 14 shows one example for the 1888 proof VAM 25 with the top of an 8 digit showing in two adjacent denticle spaces. Although Morgan proof dies received special extra polishing during the hubbing and basining/polishing steps, the date digits were also punched into the proof dies by hand just like the working dies.

MPDs In Lower Hair

Two examples of the bottom of a date digit punched into the lower hair of the Liberty head are known and are very **unusual**! Figure 15 of 1886 P VAM 21 shows the bottom curved bar of an 8 thru the designer's inital M just above the lower left side of the hair. Although known as a die gouge since Bill Fivaz reported it in 1974, it was shown by Bill Van Note in 1998 to match the curvature of the bottom of an 8 digit and thus is a misplaced date digit. Why it was punched above the date in a relatively inconspicuous place instead of the pretty well hidden denticle spaces is not known.

The other case is a 1892 O VAM 12 with the bottom of a 9 showing in the lower hair vee above the 92 digits as shown in Figure 16. It is a fairly small segment of the 9 lower loop but it matches the curvature and is a broad curved raised bar typical of most MPDs. In addition, this 1892 O variety has overlapping reeding at three different locations on the edge and a sub-variety VAM 12A shows a partial incuse clashed n next to the Liberty head neck, as illustrated in the section on MPD photographs. It is quite a **spectacular** coin variety with three different types of **interesting** variety features!

Top 100 and Hot 50 MPDs

The four **Top 100** MPD varieties listed and pictured in this Guide are:

- 1885 S VAM 9 with a quite visible 885 tops in denticle spaces and an S/S mint mark of VAM 6 that was the reason for the Top 100 listing.
- 1886 P VAM 21 with bottom of 8 below designer's initial M that was listed as VAM 1B die gouge for Top 100.
- 1888 O VAM 9 with 18-8 tops in denticle spaces and a doubled die reverse that was the reason for Top 100 listing.
- 1896 P VAM 19. With 8 top in denticle spaces that was only Top 100 listed as MPD, a blundered die.

The three **Hot 50** MPD varieties listed and pictured in this Guide are:

- 1884 O VAM 25 with 188 tops in denticle spaces and listed as Hot 50 for the MPD.
- 1888 P VAM 18 with 8 top in denticle spaces that was listed as Hot 50 for a doubled eyelid.
- 1900 P VAM 16 with 900 tops in denticle spaces and listed as Hot 50 for the 2 olive reverse with the 900 MPD mentioned.

Thus, there were one Top 100 and one Hot 50 varieties listed for the MPD feature and a second Top 50 variety that mentioned an MPD as a secondary feature. But all Top 100 and Hot 50 varieties are sought after by collectors which makes them very desirable.

Figure 11 1888 O VAM 28 1 in Denticles

Figure 12 1883 O VAM 40 1 in Denticles

Figure 13 1887 O VAM 27 7 in Denticles

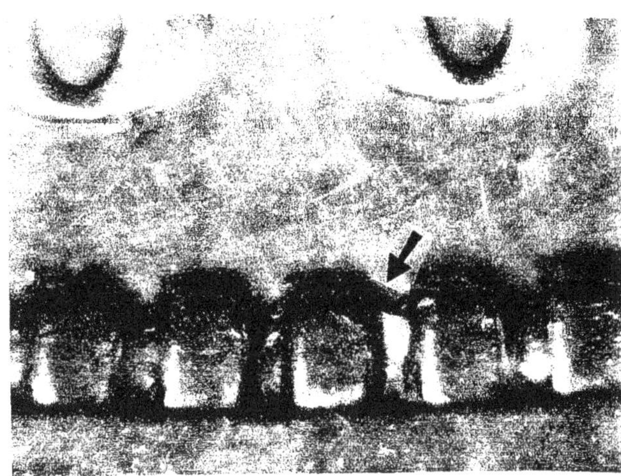

Figure 14 1888 Proof VAM 25 8 in Denticles

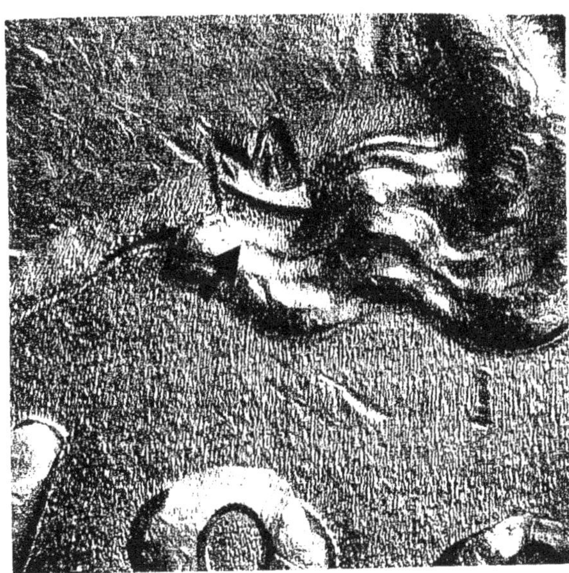

Figure 15 1886 P VAM 21 8 Below M

Figure 16 1892 O VAM 12 9 Below Hair

ATTRIBUTING THE MISPLACED DATE DIGITS VARIETIES

There are currently 56 listed MPD die varieties plus six sub-varieties that include the MPD and clashed dies with letter transfers. An accompanying **MPD Quick Attribution Summary Chart** lists the MPDs with VAM die variety numbers (Taken from the first letters of **V**an **A**llen and **M**allis who co-authored the book, *Comprehensive Catalog & Encyclopedia of Morgan & Peace Dollars*, by Leroy C. Van Allen & A. George Mallis, DLRC Press, 3rd ed. 1992 & 4th ed. printing 1998.). Also given are variety titles, desirability, short descriptions and who reported each variety on what date.

The procedure for attributing Morgan dollar MPDs is relatively simple. One approach is to first locate in the denticle spaces something that looks like a curved raised bar using a 7X or greater hand glass or 10X stereo microscope. Then the MPD Quick Attribution Summary Chart can be consulted to see if the MPD short descriptions match what is seen on that date coin or alternatively, if the photos of the MPDs in the back of this Guide match the coin features.

Another attribution approach is to consult the MPD Quick Attribution Summary Chart to determine if there are any MPDs listed for the date and mint of the coin being examined. The short summary description of any possible MPDs for the date/mint of the coin will point out what to look for as will also the MPD photos at the back of the book.

The number of **desirability stars** is given for each variety with a range of one thru five with five being the most desirable. This is a subjective number based on their visibility, number of digits showing and whether they are a Top 100 or Hot 50 variety. The factors considered for the number of desirability stars are discussed further in the section, Top 25 Misplaced Date Digits.

There are one to six MPDs listed so far for **every year** from 1879 thru 1892, plus some for 1896, 1900, 1901 &1903. All but four of the listings are for the tops of date digits that appear in the denticles below the date. There is also one listing of 1886 P VAM 21 where the bottom loop of an 8 appears below the designer's initial, M, and one listing of 1892 O VAM 12 where the bottom loop of a 9 appears below the hair to the right of the designer's initial M. The most visible MPD of the Morgan dollar series is the 1882 CC VAM 2 with a diagonal bar of 1 top below the left 8 and above the denticles. The amazing 1882 P VAM 24 shows two partial left bases of 1 in the field below the 18.

Most of the MPD listings are for the **top** of a **single** date digit in the denticles. There are 36 single-digit, five two-digits, ten three-digits and one example where the tops of all four-digits show, the 1883 O VAM 39. The 1885 S VAMs 8 & 9 share the same MPD obverse of 885 in the denticles but with different reverse dies. **Single** digit tops in the denticles are only listed if there are **raised curved bars** in **two adjacent denticle spaces**, unless the raised curved bar in a single denticle space is **unusually bold** and clear.

It was likely that a single digit punch was the most handy and easily used digit punch available to the mint worker who punched the date digits into a die. As discussed in a later section, Possible Reasons For MPDs, the tops of the date digits were possibly lightly punched into a convenient location of denticles or lower hair line near the normal date location in order to determine if the dies had been annealed. After the working dies had the design hubbed into them, they had to be annealed to soften the metal that had been work hardened by the multiple hubbing operations. Punching the date into a working die that was still hardened would have damaged the digit punches which were valuable and difficult to replace. The separation of the die annealing facility on a different floor of the Philadelphia Mint from the die engraving room probably required the occasional testing that the dies had been annealed by punching the top of a digit(s) into the denticles of a single die in the batches of 20 to 40 dies in a single die box. This is discussed in greater detail in the later section, Purposely Punched MPDs.

Only the tops of the date digits will show in the denticle spaces on the Morgan dollars because of the short length of the space. The denticles on the dies are depressed cavities and the denticle spaces are bars slightly depressed below the die fields. The die rim is depressed like the denticles. Thus, when a date digit was punched into the denticles on the die, it only contacted the denticle space or the nearby field.

There are only three Carson City Morgan dollars listed with MPDs, the 1882 CC VAM 2 with the very visible top of 1 below the left 8, the 1890 CC VAM 7 with 0 in the denticles and the 1892 CC VAM 10 with a 9 or 2 in the denticles. This was because the Carson City Mint generally struck fewer Morgan dollars each year than the other mints and also only struck Morgan dollars in 13 years of the total of 27 years that they were struck from 1878 thru 1904. Thus, the Carson City Mint used much fewer working dies than the other mints. Only 445 Carson City Morgan dollar dies were produced compared to 1,797 for San Francisco, 2,397 for Philadelphia and 2,463 for New Orleans Mints. (See page 60 in the VAM book.)

MPD QUICK ATTRIBUTION SUMMARY CHART

			Desirability	Reported By
1879 S	VAM 44	**Possible 7 in denticles**	★	Herb Zepke April 1999
		Raised straight bars in two denticle spaces below 8 and narrow vertical bar on left side of adjacent right denticle space. Doubled to sextupled left and right stars. 87 doubled at top outside.		
1880 P	VAM 51	**8 in denticles**	★★	John Coxe Oct 2007
		Raised curved bar in denticle space below 1. Doubled 880. Doubled reverse legend.		
1881 S	VAM 52	**8 in denticles**	★★★	Bill Van Note Nov 1998
		Raised curved bars in two adjacent denticle spaces below second 8.		
	VAM 53	**8 in denticles**	★★★	Bill Van Note Nov 1998
		Raised curved bars in two adjacent denticle spaces between 8's.		
	VAM 61	**Possible 1 in denticles**	★★	Jerry Robertson April 2005
		Raised squared off bar in right side of denticle space below first 8 and diagonal bar in adjacent left denticle space.		
1882 P	VAM 20	**8 in denticles**	★★★	Bill Van Note Nov 1998
		Raised curved lines in two adjacent denticle spaces between 8's. Metal in both 8's & 2. Reverse has doubled tops of In God We Trust and bottom inside of TED STATES.		
	VAM 23	**8 in denticles**	★	Norman Salter Feb 2008
		Two faint curved lines in adjacent denticle spaces between 18. Die gouges second right star. Die gouge eagle's neck over to wing.		
	VAM 24	**Double 1 base above denticles**	★★★★★	Brian Raines May 2008
		Double left side of 1 base below 18 showing as horizontal and vertical lines. Doubled 882.		
1882 CC	VAM 2	**1 Top Below Left 8**	★★★★★	Jym Braun Aug 2001
		Diagonal bar below left 8 with length and curve of 1 top. Later die states have bar polished off. Doubled 882. First reported by Charles Easterberg in Nov 1976 as polishing mark.		
	VAM 2A	**1 Top Below Left 8**	★★★★★	Michael Ash Oct 2006
		Also has clashed die with faint incuse n of In next to Liberty head neck. Diagonal bar of 1 top still shows.		
	VAM 2B	**Doubled 882**	★	George Mallis June 1965
		Polished die removing clashed n and diagonal bar of 1 top.		
	VAM 2C	**Doubled 882, Counterclash**	★★★	Laurence Galbraith Jan 2006
		Die break at back of Phrygian cap and counterclash doubled lip. No diagonal bar of 1 top.		
1883 P	VAM 4	**8 in denticles**	★★★	Bill Van Note Nov 1998
		Raised curved bar in denticle space between 8's and diagonal curved line in adjacent left denticle space. Doubled 1-83. 1 doubled below top crossbar. 83 strongly doubled at top outside.		

1883 O VAM 39 **Date digits in denticles** ★★★★★ Bill Van Note Nov 1998
Tops of digits in denticle spaces as raised straight bar below 1, raised curved bars below first 8, second 8 and to left of 3.
Die flake inside lower loop and right outside of first 8.

VAM 40 **1 in denticles** ★★★ Andrew Van Note Nov 1998
Partial top of 1 in field above denticle below first 8 and raised curved line to left between denticles.

1884 P VAM 15 **188 in denticles** ★★★★ Henry Maddocks May 2005
Raised vertical bar in denticle space below 1. Raised curved bar in denticle space below first 8 and also below second 8 with small notch in adjacent left space.
Far date.

VAM 17 **Possible 4 in denticles** ★ John Coxe Oct 2007
Raised diagonal bar in denticle space below left 8.
Die scratches E to star.

VAM 18 **Possible 8 in denticles** ★ Bill Latour Nov 2007
Raised curved bar in dent5icle space below right 8.

1884 O VAM 25 **188 in denticles** **HOT 50** ★★★★★ Bill Fivaz April 1997
Tops of digits in denticle spaces as raised straight bar below 1, raised curved bar below first 8 and raised curved bar with straight top below second 8 and short curved bar in adjacent left space.
O mint mark re-punched with curved line at bottom of opening.

VAM 37 **18 in denticles** ★★★ Bill Fivaz Feb 1997
Short vertical raised bar in denticle space between 18 and raised curved bar in denticle space below first 8.
Far date.

VAM 37A **18 in denticles** ★★★ Brent Fogelberg Oct 2004
Also has clashed die with faint incuse st of Trust from reverse showing in right hair vee of lower hair edge.
Small die chip below cap fold.

VAM 38 **Possible 8 in denticles** ★ Bill Van Note Nov 1998
Raised curved bar in denticle space between 8 and 4.
Top of 1 doubled.
O mint mark tilted left.

1884 S VAM 8 **18 in denticles** ★★★★ Bill Van Note Nov 1998
Raised vertical bar in denticle space between 18 and raised curved bars in two adjacent denticle spaces to right of first 8.
Far date. Some show tiny die chip on left side of neck point.

VAM 9 **884 in denticles** ★★★★ Bill Van Note Nov 1998
Tops of 884 in denticle spaces with raised curve bars in adjacent spaces below first 8, raised curved bar below second 8 and raised vertical bar below 4.
Far date.

1885 P VAM 28 **Possible 8 in denticles** ★ Bill Latour Nov 2007
Raised curved bar in denticle space between 85.
Far date

1885 O VAM 17 **8 in denticles** ★★ Clayton Christiansen Jan 2001
Raised curved bar in denticle space below first 8.
Far date.

1885 S VAM 8 **885 in denticles** ★★★★ Bill Van Note Nov 1998
Tops of 885 in denticle spaces with raised curved bars below first and second 8 and raised straight top bar below 5.

VAM 9 **885 in denticles** **TOP 100** ★★★★★ Herb Zepke Feb 1999
Same tops of 885 in denticle spaces as VAM 8.
S/S mint mark with vertical spike to left of lower serif, diagonal line inside upper loop.
Same as reverse as VAM 6

1886 P VAM 21 **8 below designer's initial M** Bill Fivaz Jan 1974 as die gouge, Bill Van Note Nov 1998
TOP 100 ★★★★★
Bottom of 8 as raised curved bar below designer's initial M at base of neck.
Doubled legend and motto letters plus upper leaves of right wreath.

1887 P VAM 11 **7 in denticles** ★★★ Bill Van Note Nov 1998
Raised curved bar in denticle space below 7 and raised vertical bar in right adjacent denticle space.
Doubled 18-7 with 18 doubled at bottom and 7 at top outside.

VAM 13 **7 in denticles** ★★★ Bill Van Note Nov 1998
Raised curved bar in denticle space below second 8 and short raised vertical bar in left adjacent denticle space.
Doubled first four right stars and first two left stars.
Doubled legend letters and right wreath leaves on reverse.

VAM 17 **8-7 in denticles, with double punch** ★★★★ Richard Pawley May 1998
Raised curved bars above and at field level between denticles below left 8. Raised curved bars above and at field level between denticles below 7 and vertical curved bar in adjacent right space.

VAM 19 **7 in denticles** ★★ Leroy Van Allen Mar 2002
Raised curved bar in denticle space below 7, and raised notches of bar in adjacent left space.
Very far date.

1887 O VAM 27 **7 in denticles** ★★★ Bill Van Note Nov 1998
Raised curved bar in denticle space between 87 and raised vertical bar in adjacent right space.

VAM 28 **18-7 in denticles** ★★★★ Robert Roach Feb 1998
Raised curved bar in denticle space below 18, raised curved bars in two denticle spaces to right of first 8 and short raised curved bar in denticle space below 7.
Quadrupled left stars, doubled right stars and motto.
Near date.

1888 P VAM 18 **8 in denticles** **HOT 50** ★★★★★ Crae Morton May 1998
Raised curved bar in field space between denticles below second 8 and small raised tip in adjacent right space.
Eyelid doubled at bottom.
Far date.

1888 Proof VAM 25 **8 in denticles** ★★★★ Jeff Oxman Sep 1999
Raised curved bars in two field spaces between denticles between second and third 8's.
Doubled date. 1 doubled at top left, first 8 doubled at lower left outside of lower loop, second 8 doubled at lower left outside of lower loop and third 8 doubled at top left inside of upper loop.

1888 O VAM 6 **8 in denticles** ★★ John Roberts Sep 2005
Raised curved bar in denticles space below and to right of second 8 and faint curved line in right adjacent denticle space.

VAM 9 **18-8 in denticles** **TOP 100** ★★★★★ Bill Van Note Nov 1998
Short raised tip below first 8 and short raised bar in adjacent left denticle space.
Curved bar outline in fields in denticle space to left of second 8 and below third 8.
Doubled middle outside of right wreath, ONE DOLLAR & ERICA, and tail feather.

VAM 28 **1 in denticles** ★★★ Logan McKechnie Nov 2004
Raised tip in denticle space to right of first 8 and curved bar in left adjacent denticle space.
Ear slightly doubled at right inside.

VAM 33 **8 in denticles** ★★ John Vernieri July 2008
Raised curved bar in denticle below right 8.
Die gouge in ear up thru hair.

1889 P VAM 24 **8 in denticles** ★★★ Bill Van Note Nov 1998
Raised curved bar in two denticle spaces to right of second 8.

1890 P VAM 25 **9 in denticles** ★★ Leroy Van Allen Aug 2004
Raised bar in denticle space below and to right of 9 and short raised curved bar in adjacent right denticle space.

VAM 25A **9 in denticles** ★★★ Mark Kimpton Aug 2004
Also has clashed die with partial incuse n of In from reverse next to Liberty head neck.

VAM 26 **Possible 1 in Denticles** ★ Ash Harrison July 2006
Slanted bar in denticle space below 8 with same slant as 1 top.

1890 CC VAM 7 **0 in denticles** ★★★ Bill Van Note Nov 1998
Raised curved bars in two adjacent denticle spaces below 0.
First C mint mark doubled on lower left inside.

1890 O VAM 26 **890 in denticles** ★★★★★ Bill Van Note Nov 1998
Shallow curved bar in denticle space below 8, raised curved bar in denticle space left of 9 and raised curved bar in denticle space to left of 0.

VAM 28 **Possible 0 Top in Denticles** ★★ Orville Smith July 2006
Thin curved bar at end of denticle space below 0.

VAM 28A **Possible 0 Top in Denticles** ★★ Orville Smith July 2006
Also has clashed die with partial incuse n of In from reverse next to Liberty head neck and partial incuse st of Trust from reverse showing in lower right hair vee.

1890 S VAM 2 **89 in denticles** ★★★★ Bill Van Note Nov 1998
Raised curved bar in denticle space below 8 and shallow raised curved bar in field in denticle space below 9.
S/S mint mark with broken arc in top middle of upper loop and arc in middle of lower loop.

VAM 33 **Possible 7 Top in Denticles** ★ George Powell Oct 2006
Slanted bar in denticle space between 90 with lower right end.
Far date. Possible S/S with bar in lower loop.

1891 S VAM 11 **189 in denticles** ★★★ Jym Braun Oct 1999
Raised bar in denticle space below 1, raised curved bar in denticle space below and to left of 8 and curved diagonal bar in denticle space below 9.

1892 CC VAM 10 **9 or 2 in denticles** ★★★ Bill Van Note Nov 1998
Raised curved bar in field in denticle spaces between 9 and 2.

VAM 10A **9 or 2 in denticles** ★★★ Logan McKechnie Nov 2008
Also has clashed die with partial incuse st of Trust from reverse showing in lower right hair vee.

1892 O VAM 12 **9 below hair** ★★★★★ George Peterson Nov 1998
Raised curved bar below hair to right of designer's initial M.
Edge reeding is overlapping at 3, 9 & 11 o'clock.

VAM 12A **9 below hair** ★★★★★ Leroy Van Allen Sep 2004
Also has clashed die with partial incuse n of In from reverse showing next to Liberty head neck.
Edge reeding is now overlapping at 1, 5 & 11 o'clock, from rotated die.

1896 P VAM 19 **8 in denticles** **TOP 100** ★★★★★ Chris Pilliod Oct 1990
Two raised curved bars in denticle spaces below 8.

VAM 26 **Possible 9 in Denticles** ★ David Druzisky July 2007
Raised curved bar in denticle space below 9.

1900 P VAM 16 **900 in denticles** **HOT 50** ★★★★★ Bill Van Note Nov 1998
Raised curved bars in denticle space below 9, two adjacent denticle spaces below first 0 and in denticle space to left of second 0.
2 olive reverse with extra olive to right of olive connected to olive branch.

VAM 19 **0 in denticles** ★★ Bill Van Note Dec 2004
Raised curved bar in denticle space between 00. Date in normal position.
2 olive reverse with extra olive to right of olive connected to olive branch.

1900 Proof VAM 32 **0 in denticles** ★★★ Logan McKechnie Nov 2003
Raised curved bar in denticle space between 00 and small curved tick in adjacent right denticle space.
Near Date.

1900 O VAM 46 **Possible 0 in denticles** ★ Bill Sampson May 2005
Raised curved bar in denticle space between 0's.
First 0 slightly doubled at bottom outside.
Near date.

1901 O VAM 15 **90 in denticles** ★★★ Bill Van Note Nov 1998
Raised curved bars in denticle space below 9 and in denticle space below 0.
2 olive reverse with extra olive to right of olive connected to olive branch.
III O mint mark tilted to left.

1903 S VAM 6 **903 in denticles** ★★★★★ Brent Fogelberg Oct 2008
Three raised curved bars in denticle spaces below 9, 0 & 3.
2 olive reverse with extra olive to right of olive connected to olive branch.

TOP 25 MISPLACED DATE DIGITS

The following are selected as the Top 25 MPDs based on the number of partial date digits showing, their visibility and if they are a Top 100 or Hot 50 variety. There are four MPD varieties that are Top 100 varieties and another three that are Hot 50 varieties. These are automatically highly desirable MPDs. The many other MPDs that aren't a Top 100 or Hot 50 variety are given a number of **Desirability Stars** from one to five with five being the most desirable.

The desirability number of stars is a subjective number based on the **visibility** of the MPD digit(s) showing such as the strength of the top or bottom of the digit in terms of thickness, height and amount of partial digit showing. The locations of the partial digit also affects their visibility. They can be hidden deep within the recesses of the denticle space or bold in the field above the denticle space. The recently listed 1882 CC VAM 2 with 1 top below left 8 and above the denticles is the most visible Morgan dollar MPD. Added in this revision is the 1882 P with amazing double 1 base between the denticles and 18 and the 1903 S with tops of 903 in the denticles.

Another factor affecting the desirability is the **number** of partial digits showing. They have been found with only one or up to the full four partial date digits showing. In general, the greater the number of partial digits showing, the higher the desirability.

A third factor is that all **Top 100** and **Hot 50** varieties are assigned **five** desirability stars. The following chart lists the Top 25 Morgan Dollar MPDs based on their overall desirability. The date, variety number (VAM), MPD digits location and number of Desirability stars is shown. A separate Quick Attribution Chart was previously shown and a Descriptive Listing is given later in this report.

There are thirteen MPDs with five desirability stars, and nine with four stars. The rest of the Top 25 MPDs have three stars. The MPDs listed in this report but not included in the Top 25 have slightly less desirable three or two or less stars. Several are listed as possible MPDs because their visibility is borderline to be certain that what is showing is definitely the top of a digit.

TOP 25 MORGAN DOLLAR MPDs

Date	Variety #	Digits Location	Desirability
1882 P	VAM 24	Double 1 bases below left 8	★★★★★
1882 CC	VAM 2	1 top below left 8	★★★★★
1883 O	VAM 39	Date in denticles	★★★★★
1883 O	VAM 40	1 below left 8	★★★
1884 P	VAM 15	188 in denticles	★★★★
1884 O	VAM 25	188 in denticles (**Hot 50**)	★★★★★
1884 S	VAM 8	18 below left 8	★★★★
1884 S	VAM 9	884 in denticles	★★★★
1885 S	VAM 8	885 in denticles	★★★★
1885 S	VAM 9	885 in denticles (**Top 100**)	★★★★★
1886 P	VAM 21	8 below initial M (**Top 100**)	★★★★★
1887 P	VAM 17	8-7 in denticles	★★★★
1887 O	VAM 28	18-7 in denticles	★★★★
1888 P	VAM 18	8 below second 8 (**Hot 50**)	★★★★★
1888 Proof	VAM 25	8 between 2nd & 3rd 8	★★★★
1888 O	VAM 9	18-8 in denticles (**Top 100**)	★★★★★
1890 O	VAM 26	890 in denticles	★★★★★
1890 S	VAM 2	89 below 8	★★★★
1891 S	VAM 11	189 in denticles	★★★★
1892 CC	VAM 10	9 or 2 between 92	★★★
1892 O	VAM 12	9 below hair line	★★★★★
1896 P	VAM 19	8 below 8 (**Top 100**)	★★★★★
1900 P	VAM 16	900 in denticles (**Hot 50**)	★★★★★
1901 O	VAM 15	90 in denticles	★★★
1903 S	VAM 6	903 in denticles	★★★★★

POSSIBLE REASONS FOR MPDs

An obvious possible reason for the occurrence of parts of the date digits so far below or above the normal date position, including below the Liberty head neck truncation, is a **misjudgement** in positioning of the date digit punch when punching the date into the working dies. On the other hand, perhaps the MPDs were a case of **deliberate punching** parts of the date digits in obscure places on the working dies. Both of these possibilities are examined in the following sections.

Punching Date Digits into Working Dies

But first, how were the date digits punched into the Morgan dollar working dies? In making the Morgan dollar working dies, the date digits and mint mark (for dies to be used at the branch mints) were punched in by hand at the Philadelphia Mint. This was done after the working dies had been annealed following the design hubbing steps, but before the dies were polished and hardened.

No photographs seem to exist showing the date digits being punched into the Morgan dollar working dies by a mint worker or other die preparation steps. The die manufacturing process was not shown to the general public during the time period that the Morgan dollars were struck and were considered sensitive operations. The author did witness the die manufacturing process, including the punching of a mint mark in an Eisenhower die during a tour of the Philadelphia Mint in 1978. The process of punching the date into the Morgan dollar working dies would have been similar. Figure 17 shows a mint worker punching the mint mark into an Eisenhower die. The dies were individually clamped into a jeweler's vise with the die in a vertical position, die face at the top and the design in the normal upright position. The mint mark was held in the right hand in a vertical position and carefully lowered against the die face and lined up in position by eye. Three quick taps within less than a second were given to the punch using a double headed 12 ounce hammer. A quick visual inspection with the naked eye was given to the mint mark to determine if it was of deep enough impression and of proper placement and orientation.

Figure 18 shows the mint mark punches used in the 1970's which would have been similar to individual date digit punches used on the Morgan dollar. Also shown are specimen pieces that are copper blanks struck on one side to show for each coin denomination the preferred mint mark position and orientation. It is not known if specimen pieces or drawings were used as guides for the date placement on Morgan dollars.

The date position of the Morgan dollar was fixed for the years 1878 thru 1883 but varied in lateral, vertical and orientation positions from 1884 thru 1904 (See page 114 in the VAM book). For 1878, the complete date was in the master die and working dies and didn't vary in position.

During 1879 the 187 digits were in a **fixed** position on the hub with the 9 punched into the working dies with a four digit logotype or single digit punch. In 1880, both right digits were removed from the master hub. From 1880 thru 1883 the first two digits, 18, **were on the working hubs** and the last two digits were punched into each working die using a four or two digit logotype or a single digit punch.

The date digits were made slightly smaller in 1884. The **complete** dates were punched into each working die by hand, again using two or four digit logotype and single digit punches from 1884 thru 1904 causing the date positions to vary. For the 1921 Morgan dollar, the date digits were in the master die and their working dies all had the same date position.

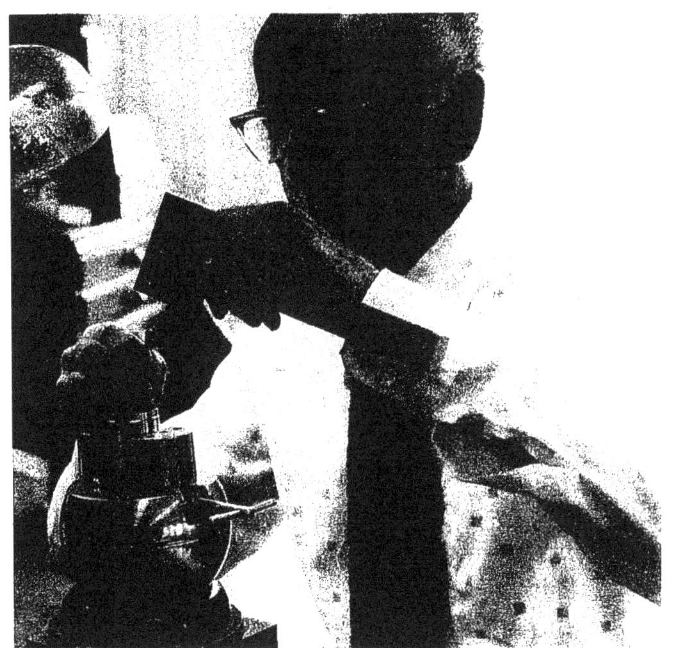

Figure 17 Punching Mint Mark Into Die, 1970 s

Figure 18 Mint Mark Punches & Specimen Pieces, 1970 s

Figure 19 1883 P VAM 2 Dash Under 8

Blundered Dies?

Since the first date digits, 18, were in a **fixed** position in all working dies from the hubbing operation from 1880 thru 1883, it would seem highly unlikely that any added date digit would be punched very far out of position. Yet, the tops of an 8 digit have been found in the denticle spaces below the second 8 or between the 8's for 1881, 1882 and 1883. Amazingly, the tops of all four date digits appear in the denticle spaces below the date on an 1883 O die. How could a four digit punch be mis-located so far off when the 18 cavities were in the die? In addition, an 1883 O die shows the top of a 1 in the denticles below the first 8 and no other digit tops. The 1882 CC VAM 2 shows the top of a 1 below the left 8 and above the denticles. How could the single digit of 1 be so far mis-punched when the 1 cavity was already in the die and why would only a single 1 digit be used? The recently reported 1882 P VAM 24 shows two partial bases of 1 in the field below the 18 that had the 1 punch tilted to the left. Only the left side of the 1 bases shows below the left 8. How could the 1 digit punch be mis-positioned so far to the right and down, plus tilted, not once but twice?

Because of the broad round bottom of the 8, a **short dash** was often marked on a working die just above the tenth denticle to the right of the Liberty head neck vee. Figure 19 shows an example of a dash below the second 8 for an 1883 P VAM 2. This was an index mark to position the second 8 in the date and are seen on numerous dies from 1879 thru 1886. These dash index marks were sometimes used in 1884 thru 1886 when it was abandoned because the smaller date digits using this index mark resulted in the left edge of the 1 base being further from the neck vee than the previous standard over the third denticle. There is no known example of a MPD occurring in combination with this dash index mark. Is this a coincidence or is there a reason the 24 known MPDs from 1879 thru 1886 didn't occur with a dash index mark? More on this later.

A strange thing about the MPDs from 1879 thru 1883 is that of the twelve known examples, only one MPD shows the last right date digit, an 1883 O that shows the tops of all four date digits. All the other MPDs show a single MPD digit of a 1, 8 or 7 but none of the last right digit. If a complete date was being punched into a working die, then a blundered punch of the date into the denticles should have shown the last right digit more consistently.

There are 43 known examples of MPDs from 1884 thru 1901 with the 1885 S VAMs 8 & 9 sharing the same obverse die but with different reverse dies. Possibly 18 of these include the last right date digit. The rest only include one, two or three tops of the first three left date digits. Why didn't all the MPDs show the last right digit if a blundered punch of the date was made into the denticles?

It is also strange that each of the six known MPDs for 1887 show the last right 7 digit in the denticles. But for the thirteen known MPDs of the years 1888 thru 1892, only possibly five MPDs show the top of the last right digit. Perhaps the top of the 7 show consistently in 1887 die denticles because it was a fairly straight horizontal bar that would show up better in the denticles than a rounded top of 8 or 9.

There have been MPDs reported for every year from 1879 thru 1892. There is a gap of MPDs for 1893, 1894 & 1895, which had net mintage of three million or less each year of the Morgan dollar. Prior year's mintage were 23 to 38 million each year except for 1892 which was six million. The MPDs reported so far after the three low mintage years are 1896, 1900, 1901 and 1903 which each had a total mintage of over 20 million, except the 1903 which had 10 million. Would blundered date punches on one to six dies appear **consistently** each year for 14 straight high mintage years? Or was there another possible reason the tops or bottoms of the digits appeared above or below the date?

If the date digits were mistakenly punched around the intended position, most of the date digits would appear **close** to the normal position with **fewer** appearing **further** away from the normal position. Most of the many misplaced digits of blundered dies of other series listed by Breen show in the field of the coin above or below the date. This is what would be expected if the date was accidently punched out of the normal position.

For the Morgan dollar, basining (Grinding the face of a die on a rotating disc with a compound to produce a desired radius of curvature.) and polishing of the obverse working dies would remove much of the evidence of misplaced date digits in the field, if they weren't as deep as the final date digits. Or the die may have been destroyed if it wasn't salvageable. There are a few examples known of the Morgan dollar with fairly widely separated date punches, but only two appearing in the field near the denticles and two in the lower hair line. Could the date digits have been purposely punched into the denticles or lower hairline?

Purposely Punched MPDs?

It certainly is a strange **coincidence** that every year from 1879 thru 1892 have one to six known examples of MPDs. These were all high mintage years, except 1892. Were they purposely created for a reason and, if so, why would the Philadelphia Mint create flaws on a working die?

Why would partial date digits be purposely punched in obscure locations above and below the date? There was no need to show partial date digits in conjunction with a full date on just a fraction of the total working dies produced. It possibly could have been done as some sort of **testing** of a die. The most logical testing would have been to determine if the dies were **annealed** after the hubbing operations to remove the **work hardening** and before the **final hardening**.

Although the date digit punches were of hardened steel rod, they would have been damaged if struck with a hammer blow against the field of a work hardened die from the hubbing operations or the final hardened die. The date digit punches were valuable and likely of a very limited number. Making new date punches of a specific size and design would have been a time consuming task. The date digit punches, therefore, had to always be punched into softened or annealed working dies.

A Likely Reason for MPDs

The Philadelphia Mint prepared working dies in **batches** with each working die hubbed 7 to 10 times and annealed between each hub blow. Figure 20 shows the boxes of dies on the bench and floor of the medal room in the Philadelphia Mint in 1901. Figure 21 shows the die room of the Philadelphia Mint in 1901 with the lathes and a screw press. The Philadelphia Mint still processes the working dies in batches of 20 to 40 in a box, depending on the die size, as shown in Figure 22 at a die inspection station in the 1970's. Accompanying each box of dies in the 1970's was a die processing sign-off card shown in Figure 23 that had sign-off lines for the various die processing steps such as hubbing, annealing, polishing, mint mark addition, inspection and hardening. It is not known if similar die processing sign-off cards were used during the production of Morgan dollar dies.

It's possible that the engraving department personnel working with Morgan dollar dies needed to be **certain** that a batch of working dies had been annealed before punching the full date into them. Up until the new Philadelphia Mint was introduced in 1901, the die annealing and hardening room was located far away on a different floor than where the dies had the date punched into the dies in the engraving room. One way to test if the dies had been annealed would have been to lightly tap a single or number of digits punch into a obscure location in the denticles or lower hairline to determine if shallow impressions were made with the top or bottom of digit(s) to indicate an annealed die. It would not have mattered if the last digit wasn't always used, which would have been missing on the 1879 thru 1883 working dies that had the first two or three left digits already in them. Any convenient date digit(s) could have been used to test the dies below the date. Possibly even date digit punches of different denominations or letters could have been used. Also, the lateral position and orientation would not have been critical so long as the punched digit was somewhat under the normal date position. The known MPDs show this convenient selection of various date digits and are not always aligned directly below or above the correct digit positions.

A **likely reason** for the misplaced partial date digits in the denticles or lower hairlines could therefore have been to **test the hardness** of a batch of working dies to determine if they were **annealed** before punching in a full date. Only **one** die would have needed to be tested in a batch of dies. Thus,

Figure 20 Medal Room, Philadelphia Mint, 1901, Die Boxes on Bench & Floor
George Morgan wielding hammer

Figure 21 Die Room, Philadelphia Mint, 1901

the hardness could have been tested for each year when a high volume of working dies were made and the annealing status may have been in question for some batches of dies.

Annealing of Dies

The dies were annealed after the hubbing operations which work hardened them by the displacement of metal on the die face. The dies were put in an iron pot and packed with carbon to exclude the air. They were heated to a bright red and allowed to cool very gradually as described in the *Annual Report of the Director of the Mint*, 1896, page 151 and *Visitors Guide to The U.S. Mint Philadelphia,* 1885, page 26.

There are no available photographs of Morgan dollar dies being annealed, but the process was still similar to that used by the Philadelphia Mint in the 1970's. In this later time, each die was placed face down in a Nichrome crucible cup as shown in Figure 24 and packed with charcoal around it to prevent pitting and decarbonization by the oxygen in the air. Twenty-five of these crucibles were in turn placed in a large pot filled with charcoal and a cover put over the whole assembly as shown in Figure 25. This assembly was placed in a gas fired furnace shown in Figure 26. The dies were heated and maintained at a temperature of 1,400° to 1,450°F over a period of five hours and then allowed to cool slowly for eight hours.

This die annealing process was an entirely different step and process than the die hardening step after the date and mint mark had been punched into the die. The working dies were hardened to greatly prolong their life in striking the relatively soft silver-copper alloy of the Morgan dollar planchets or blanks. For the Morgan dies, a mask of fixed oil or oil thickened with animal charcoal, or of lampblack and linseed oil was put on the die face. They were then placed, face downward, in a crucible with animal charcoal and heated to cherry-red. Each die was then plunged into a large tank of water and kept in rapid motion until cooled. If there was any piping or singing sounds, it indicated a crack or other imperfection and the die was destroyed. (As related in *Visitors Guide to The U.S. Mint Philadelphia*, page 26.) Figure 27 shows the furnace for die hardening in the 1970's with each die again packed face down in charcoal in a Nichrome crucible cup. They were heated up to 1,500°F with an hour's heating duration per inch of die diameter. Each die was then individually thrust into an 8 to 10 percent brine tank and moved vigorously around until all bubbling action ceased as shown in Figure 28.

Hardening of the dies leaves them with internal stresses which can lead to pre-mature cracks and chips. To relieve these stresses, the dies were tempered which is an entirely different operation than the previously discussed annealing step. In the 1896 *Annual Director of The Mint Report* of the words of engraver, Charles E. Barber, "...the temper is... done by gently heating until you notice a color appearing on the surface of the steel... to a deeper color (than light straw) and in some cases to a blue." In the 1970's the dies were placed loose in batches in a special die tempering furnace and heated to 400°F for two hours as shown in Figures 29 and 30.

Figure 22 Die Inspection Station with Box of Dies, 1970 s

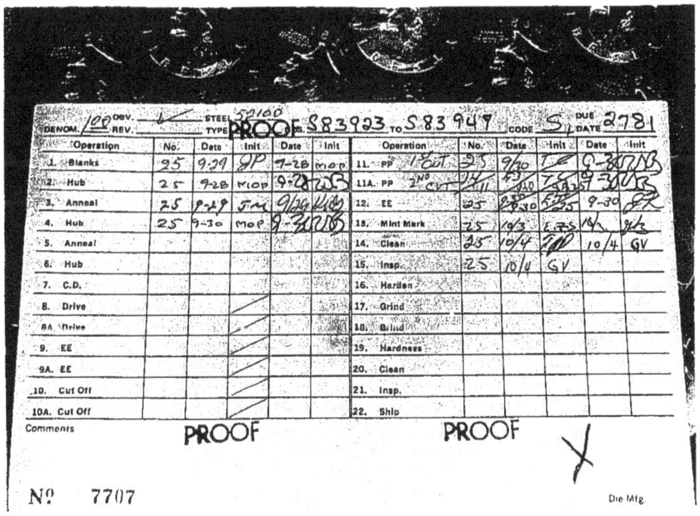

DENOM. 100 OBV. REV. STEEL TYPE 52100 PROOF S83923 TO S83949 CODE S DUE DATE 2781

Operation	No.	Date	Init	Date	Init	Operation	No.	Date	Init	Date	Init
1. Blanks	25	9-29	JP	9-28	MOP	11. PP 1st CUT	25	9/30			
2. Hub	25	9-28	MOP			11A. PP 2nd CUT					
3. Anneal	25	9-29		9/29		12. EE	25			9-30	
4. Hub	25	9-30	MOP			13. Mint Mark	25	10/3			
5. Anneal						14. Clean	25	10/4		10/4	GV
6. Hub						15. Insp.	25	10/4	GV		
7. C.D.						16. Harden					
8. Drive						17. Grind					
8A. Drive						18. Grind					
9. EE						19. Hardness					
9A. EE						20. Clean					
10. Cut Off						21. Insp.					
10A. Cut Off						22. Ship					

Comments PROOF PROOF

Nº 7707 Die Mfg.

Figure 23 Die Processing Sign-Off Card, 1970 s

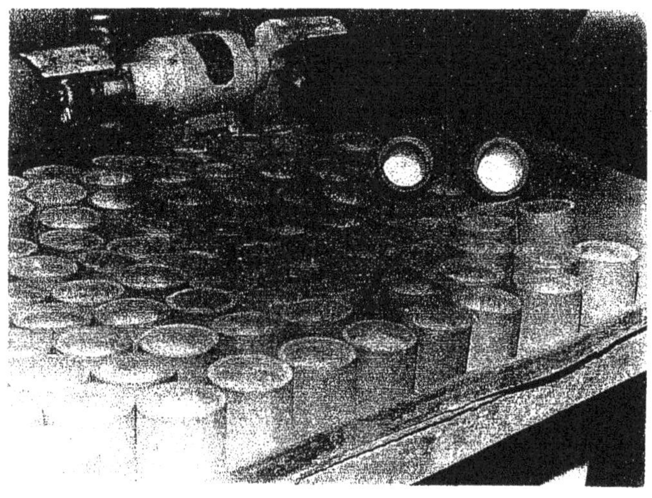

Figure 24 Nichrome Crucibles to Hold Dies, 1970's

Figure 25 Crucibles & Dies Packed in Charcoal, 1970's

Figure 26 Die Annealing Furnace
with Dies in Pots, 1970's

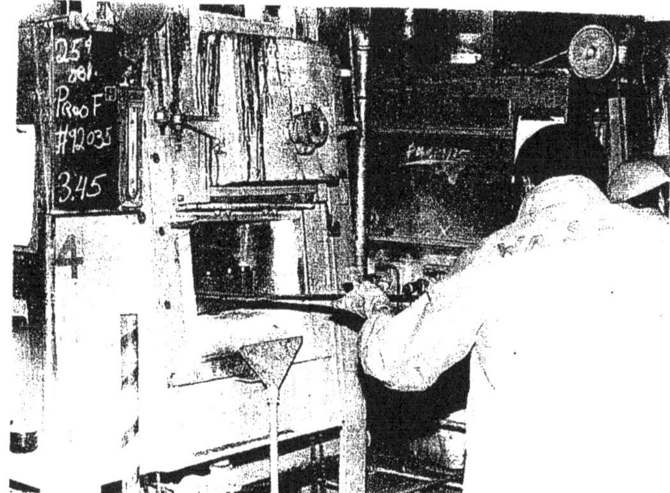

Figure 27 Furnace for Die Hardening, 1970's

Figure 28 Quenching Dies in a Brine Vat, 1970's

Some Final Conclusions

When a **dash** was put above the tenth right denticle from the Liberty head neck vee, that would have indicated that a die had been annealed. There would not have been any need to punch the tops of digits into denticles if punching a dash above the tenth denticle had already indicated the die was annealed. That is the case, as no MPDs have been found when dashes were present below the date from 1879 through 1886.

In addition, there are many known MPDs that are not of the last right date digit, which was always missing on the Morgan dollar working dies after 1878. How could any of the three left digits be accidently punched into the denticles without the **last** right digit also showing? And why aren't more digits found in the **field** around the date or some of the bottom or middle parts of the digits showing in the denticles if the date was mistakenly punched too low? The possible answer is that the **tops** of the date digit(s) fit onto the slightly depressed denticle spaces as a **convenient area** to lightly tap the digit punches to determine if the dies were **annealed**.

Another interesting finding is that only one MPD, the 1903 S, have been found for the Morgan dollars on the **later** years of 1902 through 1904. This was likely due to the introduction of the new Philadelphia Mint sometime in 1901. All new equipment was installed in the engraver's department and the die annealing and hardening room was then located on the **same** floor and adjoining the die room instead of on a different floor of the previous mint. (*Annual Report of the Director of the Mint*, 1902, U.S. Treasury Department, page 125). Thus, the new equipment and procedures introduced in the engraver's department in 1901 could have **eliminated** the need to check the hardness of a batch of working dies by punching the top of date digit(s) into the die denticles. The 1903 S MPD could have been an isolated case of a batch of dies whose annealing status was uncertain and a quick test punch was made with the 903 logotype in the denticles.

Figure 29 Die Tempering Furnaces, 1970 s

Figure 30 Dies in Tempering Furnace, 1970 s

MISPLACED DATE DIGITS DESCRIPTIVE LISTINGS

1879 S

44 **III^{2}22 • C^{3}a (Possible 7 in Denticles, Doubled 87, Sextupled Stars)** **(179)** **I-3** **R-5**

Obverse III^{2}22– Possible top of 7 showing in denticles as raised straight bars in two denticles spaces below 8 and narrow vertical bar on left side of adjacent right denticle space. Top outside of 8 and 7 slightly doubled. All left and right stars doubled to sextupled towards rim.

1880 P

51 **III^{2}50 • C^{3}d (Doubled 880, 8 in Denticles, Doubled Reverse Legend)** **(180)** **I-3** **R-6**

Obverse III^{2}50– Slightly doubled lower left outside of upper loop of both 8's. 0 doubled at bottom and top left inside with raised dot on left side. Top of 8 shows as raised curved bar in denticle space below 1 with slight shallow cured bar at two denticle spaces to right under left 8. Curved line in denticle space between 8's. Diagonal die scratch at jaw-neck junction near hair.

Reverse C^{3}a– Slightly doubled bottom inside of legend letters towards rim and some leaves in both wreaths.

1881 S

52 **III^{2}28 • C^{3}a (8 in Denticles)** **(185)** **I-3** **R-3**

Obverse III^{2}28– Top of 8 showing in two adjacent denticle spaces below second 8 as two raised and curved bars.

53 **III^{2}29 • C^{3}a (8 in Denticles)** **(186)** **I-3** **R-3**

Obverse III^{2}29– Top of 8 showing in denticles as raised curved bars in two adjacent denticle spaces between 8's.

61 **III^{2}35 • C^{3}a (Possible 1 in Denticles)** **(186)** **I-2** **R-5**

Obverse III^{2}35– Possible top of 1 showing in denticle spaces below first 8 as raised squared off bar on right side and a diagonal bar in adjacent left denticle space that matches diagonal of 1 top left. (Similar to 1888 O VAM 28 with 1 in denticles.)

1882 P

20 **III^{2}20 • C^{3}b (8 in Denticles, Metal in Date, Doubled Upper Reverse)** **(176)** **I-4** **R-6**

Obverse III^{2}20– Top of 8 showing in two adjacent denticle spaces between 8's as two raised and curved lines. Metal in both 8's and 2 similar to VAM 1C.

Reverse C^{3}b– Doubled tops of In God We Trust and slightly on bottom insides of TED STATES.

23 **III^{2}22 • C^{3}a (8 In Denticles)** **(180)** **I-3** **R-5**

Obverse III^{2}22– Top of 8 showing in two adjacent denticle spaces between 18 as two raised and curved lines. Two short die scratches from denticles at second right star. Late die states show die cracks around 5 & 6 right stars with break from fifth star to hair.

Reverse C^{3}a– Die gouge on lower right side of eagle's neck over to eagle's left wing edge. (Formerly VAM 1E.)

24 **III^{2}23 • C^{3}a (Doubled 882, Double 1 Base Above Denticles MPD)** **(181)** **I-5** **R-6**

Obverse III^{2}23– Doubled 882 in date. Slightly doubled left 8 at left inside and rt outside of upper loop, right 8 at left outside of both loops and 2 at top outside of upper loop. Double left side of 1 base below left 8 with narrow horizontal bar and faint vertical line at right end directly below 8 in field above denticles and another horizontal bar and stronger vertical line on right side in upper denticle space just to left of 1 base in field. 1 was punched into denticles with tilt to left, so only left base shows. Hair above date is over polished.

1882 CC

2(revised) **III^{2}2 • C^{3}b (Doubled 882, 1 Top Below Left 8)** **(178)** **I-5** **R-4**

Obverse III^{2}2– Doubled 882 in date. Slightly doubled left 8 at right outside of upper loop and left inside of lower loop and 2 at top outside. Right 8 strongly doubled on left outside of upper loop and slightly on bottom outside of lower loop. Early die states show diagonal bar below left 8 with length and slight curve of top of 1 and diagonal ends that match 1 top shape and polishing lines below first two right stars and at wheat leaves top. Raised dots in left 8 upper loop and on right 8 upper loop left surface.

Reverse C^{3}b– Polishing roughness around left star, UNITED, and STATES OF. Some doubled leaves in left wreath and bottom of right wreath. Slight doubling at top of STATES OF.

2A **III^{2}2 • C^{3}b (Doubled 882, 1 Top Below Left 8, Clashed Obverse n)** **(178)** **I-5** **R-5**

Obverse III^{2}2– Clashed die with faint partial n of In from reverse showing next to Liberty head neck.

2B **III^{2}2 • C^{3}b (Doubled 882)** **(177)** **I-2** **R-5**

Obverse III^{2}2– Die has been polished removing die clash n and polishing lines at right stars and diagonal bar of 1 top MPD below left 8.

2C **III^{2}2 • C^{3}b (Doubled 882, Die Break Back of Cap)** **(177)** **I-3** **R-5**

Obverse III^{2}2– Clashed die that has been polished. Small die break at back of Phrygian cap from die clashing. Doubled upper lip from counterclash.

1883 P

4(revised) **III^{2}4 • C^{3}a (Doubled 1-83, 8 in Denticles)** **(180)** **I-4** **R-4**

Obverse III^{2}4– Strongly doubled 1-83 in date. 1 doubled below top crossbar and at top right. 83 strongly doubled at top left and right outside. Second 8 also doubled at top right outside of lower loop and 3 doubled at top of lower serif and bottom left inside of lower loop. Top of 8 shows in denticle space between 8's as raised curved bar and in adjacent left denticle space as diagonal curved line on right side.

1883 O

39 **III^{2}22 • C^{3}a (Date Digits in Denticles, Die Flake in 8)** (181) I-5 R-4

Obverse III^{2}22– Tops of date digits showing in denticle spaces as short straight bar in denticles below 1, curved bars in denticles below first 8, second 8 and to left of 3. Die flake in lower loop of first 8 and under lower loop on right outside. Top and rear of Phrygian cap slightly doubled as is right wheat leaf.

40 **III^{2}23 • C^{3}a (1 in Denticles)** (181) I-3 R-4

Obverse III^{2}23– Partial top of 1 showing in field above denticle below first 8 and raised curved line to left of this between the denticles.

1884 P

15 **III^{2}14 • C^{3}a (188 in Denticles, Far Date)** (?) I-4 R-5

Obverse III^{2}14– Tops of 188 showing in denticles with raised vertical bar on left side of space between denticles below 1, raised curved bar in denticle space below first 8 and raised curved bar in denticle space below second 8 with small notch in adjacent left denticle space. Date set further right than normal.

17 **III^{2}16 • C^{3}a (Possible 4 in Denticles, Die Scratches E)** (?) I-3 R-5

Obverse III^{2}16– Possible top of 4 showing in denticles as diagonal raised bar in denticle space to left of left 8. Three diagonal die scratches between sixth left star and E plus long horizontal die scratch on Liberty head forehead.

18 **III^{2}17 • C^{3}a (Possible 8 in Denticles, Far Date)** (189) I-3 R-5

Obverse III^{2}17– Possible top of 8 showing in denticles showing as raised curved bar in denticle space below 8. Date set further right than normal.

1884 O

25(revised) **III^{2}15 • C^{3}p (O/O Centered Low, 188 in Denticles)** **<u>HOT 50</u>** (181) I-5 R-3

Obverse III^{2}15– Tops of 188 showing in denticles as raised straight bar between denticles below 1. Raised curved bar in denticle space below first 8. Raised curved bar with straight top between denticles below second 8, and short curved bar in next left denticle space.

Reverse C^{3}p– II O mint mark tilted left, re-punched with original showing as a curved line centered at bottom of opening.

37(revised) **III^{2}14 • C^{3}a (18 in Denticles, Far Date)** (181) I-3 R-4

Obverse III^{2}14– Tops of 18 showing in denticles as short vertical raised bar on left side of denticle space between 18. Raised curved bar in denticle space below first 8. Date set further right than normal.

37A **III^{2}14 • C^{3}a (18 in Denticles, Far Date, Clashed Obverse st)** (181) I-3 R-6

Obverse III^{2}14– Clashed die with faint partial incuse st of Trust from reverse showing in right hair vee of lower hair edge. Die crack from rim thru first U in UNUM to cap and over to LIBERTY with small die chip below cap fold.

38(revised) **III^{2}22 • C^{3}t (Doubled 1, O Tilted Left, Possible 8 in Denticles)** (181) I-2 R-3

Obverse III^{2}22– Doubled 1 at top left stronger than VAM 3. Date set further right than normal. Slightly doubled top of Phrygian cap and bottom inside of US UNUM letters towards rim. Raised curved bar between denticles below 8 & 4 that possibly could be top of 8. (Former VAM 38 became VAM 25 revised.)

1884 S

8(revised) **III^{2}4 • C^{3}b (18 in Denticles, Far Date, S Set Left)** (187) I-4 R-5

Obverse III^{2}4– Tops the 18 showing in denticles as raised vertical bar on left side of space between denticles between 18. Raised curved bars in two adjacent denticle spaces to right of first 8. Date set further right than normal. Some specimens show a tiny die chip on left side of neck point.

9 **III^{2}5 • C^{3}a (884 in Denticles, Far Date)** (?) I-4 R-5

Obverse III^{2}5– Tops of 884 showing in denticles as raised curved bars in adjacent denticle spaces below first 8, raised curved bar in denticle space below second 8 and raised vertical bar in denticle space below 4. Date set further right than normal.

1885 P

28 **III^{2}25 • C^{3}a (Possible 8 in Denticles, Far Date)** (?) I-2 R-5

Obverse III^{2}25– Possible top of 8 showing in denticle space between 8 & 5 as raised curved bar. Date set further right than normal.

Reverse C^{3}a– Very slightly doubled lower edges of a arrow shaft and feathers.

1885 O

17 **III^{2}12 • C^{3}a (8 in Denticles, Far Date)** (181) I-2 R-5

Obverse III^{2}12– Top of 8 shows in denticle space below first 8 as raised curved bar. Date set further right than normal.

1885 S

8 **III^{2}7 • C^{3}a (885 in Denticles)** (185) I-4 R-3

Obverse III^{2}7– Tops of 885 showing in denticles as raised curved bars in single denticle space below first 8 and in single denticle space below second 8, and as raised straight top bar in single denticle space below 5.

9 **III^{2}7 • C^{3}b (885 in Denticles, S/S)** **<u>TOP 100</u>** (185) I-5 R-5

Reverse C^{3}b– Same S/S as VAM 6.

1886 P

21(revised) **III^{2}20 • C^{3}c (8 Below Designer's Initial, Doubled Reverse)** **<u>TOP 100</u>** (189) I-5 R-4

Obverse III^{2}20– Bottom of 8 showing as raised curve bar below designer's initial M at base of neck. Top curve of bar has smaller radius than bottom matching the bottom inside of the 8.

Reverse C^{3}c– Doubled TED STATES OF AMERICA AR, In God We Trust, right star and upper leaves of right wreath doubled towards rim.

1887 P

11(revised) **III^{2}11 • C^{3}a (Doubled 18–7, 7 in Denticles)** **(189)** **I-3** **R-3**

Obverse III^{2}11– Doubled 18 and 7 in date. The 1 and first 8 are doubled all across the bottom. 7 doubled at top. The first 8 has a die chip between the loops on the left in some specimens. Top of 7 showing in denticles as raised curved bar in denticle space below 7 and raised vertical bar in adjacent denticle space to right.

13(revised) **III^{2}13 • C^{3}b (Doubled Stars, 7 in Denticles, Doubled Reverse)** **(190)** **I-3** **R-5**

Obverse III^{2}13– First four stars on right and first two stars on left doubled at bottom with first two on right showing strong shifts. Slight doubling on designer's initials and lower hair. Top of 7 showing in denticles as raised curved bar in denticle space below second 8 and short raised vertical bar in adjacent denticle space to left. Possible 7 in denticles.

Reverse C^{3}b– Doubled STATES OF AMERICA , right star and edges of some leaves of right wreath towards rim.

17 **III^{2}16 • C^{3}a (8-7 in Denticles)** **(?)** **I-4** **R-3**

Obverse III^{2}16– Tops of 8-7 showing in denticles as raised curved bars above and at field level between denticles below first 8. Raised curved bars above and at field level between denticles below 7 and vertical curved bar in adjacent denticle space to right. A double punch of 8 – 7 in denticles.

19 **III^{2}18 • C^{3}a (7 in Denticles, Very Far Date)** **(190)** **I-2** **R-5**

Obverse III^{2}18– Top of 7 shown in denticles as raised curved bar in denticle space below 7 and raised notched bar in adjacent denticle space to left. Date set much further right than normal but close to far date position.

1887 O

27 **III^{2}23 • C^{3}a (7 in Denticles)** **(?)** **I-3** **R-4**

Obverse III^{2}23– Top of 7 showing in denticles as raised curved bar in denticle space between 87 and raised vertical bar in an adjacent denticle space to right.

28 **III^{2}24 • C^{3}a (Doubled Stars and Motto, 18-7 in Denticles, Near Date)** **(181)** **I-4** **R-5**

Obverse III^{2}24– A doubled die in the radial direction with quadrupled to doubled left stars, slightly doubled right stars and E PLURIBUS UNUM doubled towards rim. Front of headband and forehead slightly doubled. Date set further left than normal. Tops of 18 – 7 showing in denticles as raised curved bar in denticle space below 18, raised curved bars in two denticle spaces to right of first 8 and short raised curved bar in denticle space below 7.

1888 P

18(revised) **III^{2}14 • C^{3}a (Doubled Eyelid, 8 in Denticles, Far Date)** **<u>HOT 50</u>** **(190)** **I-5** **R-4**

Obverse III^{2}14– Eyelid strongly doubled at bottom. Hair above ear, right inside and bottom outside of ear and bottom edge of lower cotton leaf are slightly doubled. Top of 8 shows in denticles as raised curved bar in field space between denticles below second 8 and small raised tip in right adjacent denticle space. Date set further right than normal.

1888 Proof

25 **III^2 20 • C^{3}a (Doubled Date, 8 in Denticles)** **(?)** **I-4** **Proof**

Obverse III^{2}20– Entire date strongly doubled to left. 1 is doubled strongly at top left as vertical bar, slightly at left top of lower cross bar and as thin line at lower left of lower cross bar. First 8 doubled strongly at lower left outside of lower loop as a curved bar. Second 8 doubled strongly at lower left outside of lower loop. Third 8 doubled slightly at top left inside of upper loop. Top of 8 showing in denticles as raised curved bars in two field spaces between denticles between second and third 8's.

1888 O

6(revised) **III^{2}5 • C^{3}a (Doubled 88 Top, Oval O, 8 in Denticles)** **(181)** **I-3** **R-5**

Obverse III^{2}5– Second 8 slightly doubled at top outside and last 8 strongly doubled at top outside as curved line separated from top. 8 showing in denticles as raised curved bar in denticle space below and to right of second 8 and faint vertical curved line in right adjacent denticle space.

9(revised) **III^{2}15 • C^{3}e (Doubled Wreath, 18-8 in Denticles)** **<u>TOP 100</u>** **(181)** **I-5** **R-5**

Obverse III^{2}15– Top of 18 – 8 showing and denticles as short raised tip on denticle below first 8 and short raised bar in adjacent left denticle space. Outline of curved bar in fields between denticles in space to left of second 8 and below third 8.

Reverse C^{3}e– Doubled lower reverse with middle outside of right wreath strongly doubled. Top inside of ONE DOLLAR and bottom inside of ERICA letters doubled. Right star doubled on left side. Bottom of eagle's tail feathers, arrow shafts and olive leaves slightly doubled. III O mint mark.

28 **III^{2}17 • C^{3}a (Doubled Ear, 1 in Denticles)** **(?)** **I-3** **R-5**

Obverse III^{2}17– Ear slightly doubled at right inside. Top of 1 showing in denticles as raised tip in denticle space to right of first 8 and curved bar in left adjacent space below first 8. Date at right edge of normal position.

33 **III^{2}22 • C^{3}a (8 in Denticles, Die Gouge Hair to Ear)** **(181)** **I-3** **R-6**

Obverse III^{2}22– 8 showing in denticles as raised curved bar in denticle space below right 8. Long diagonal die gouge from inside ear up thru hair behind eye.

1889 P

24(revised) **III^{2}22 • C^{3}a (8 in Denticles, Doubled Ear, Polishing Lines in Cotton Bolls)** **(190)** **I-3** **R-5**

Obverse III^{2}22– Top of 8 showing in denticles as raised curved bar in two denticle spaces to right of right 8. Ear slightly doubled at right inside, top right outside and bottom outside. Date in normal position. *Diagnostic–* Heavy diagonal polishing lines in cotton bolls and leaves. Same die as VAM 35.

1890 P

25 **III^{2}24 • C^{3}a (9 in Denticles)** **(189)** **I-2** **R-4**

Obverse III^{2}24– Top of 9 showing in denticles as a raised bar in denticle space below and to right of 9 and a short raised

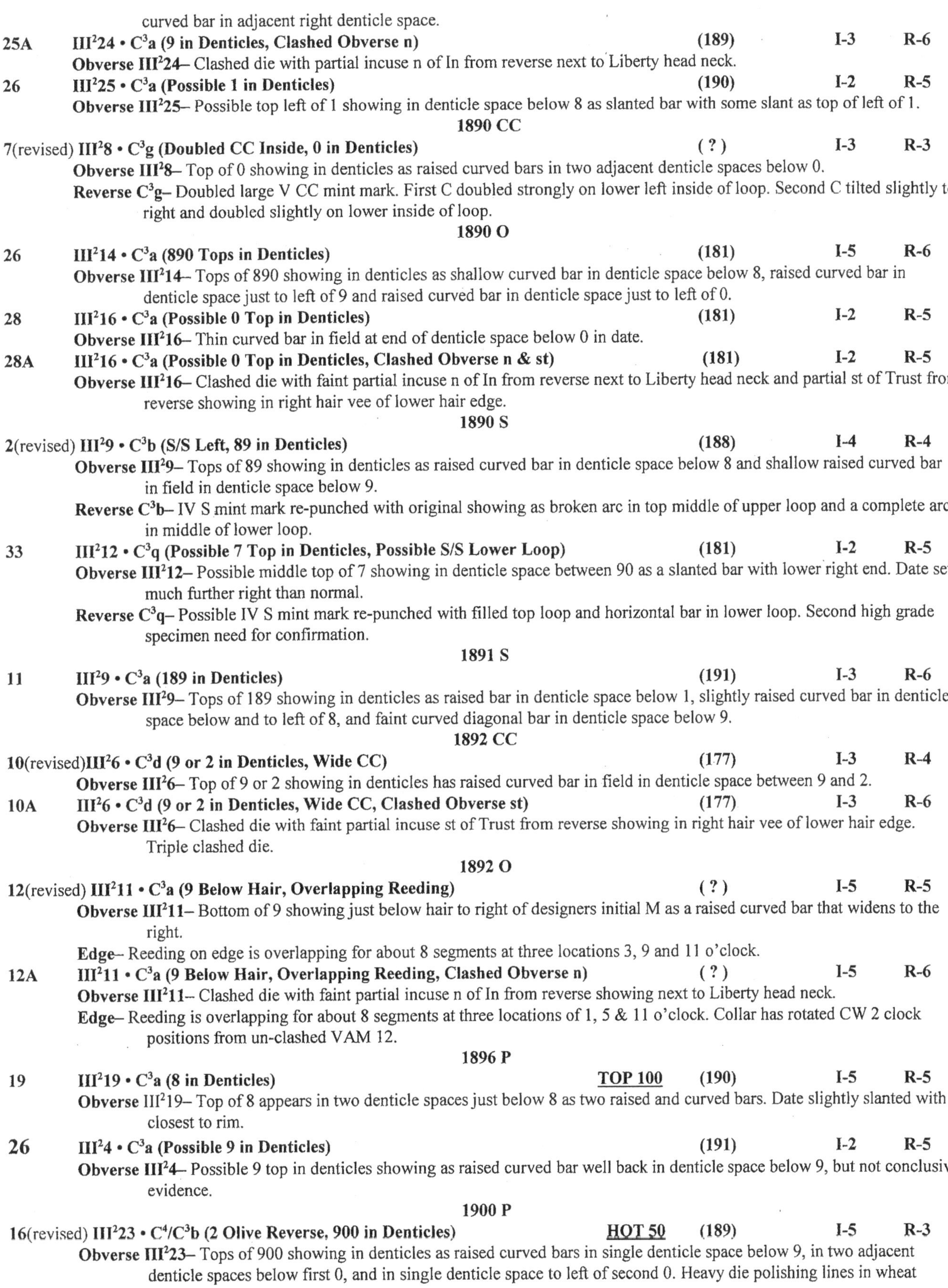

curved bar in adjacent right denticle space.

25A **III^{2}24 • C^{3}a (9 in Denticles, Clashed Obverse n)** (189) I-3 R-6

Obverse III^{2}24– Clashed die with partial incuse n of In from reverse next to Liberty head neck.

26 **III^{2}25 • C^{3}a (Possible 1 in Denticles)** (190) I-2 R-5

Obverse III^{2}25– Possible top left of 1 showing in denticle space below 8 as slanted bar with some slant as top of left of 1.

1890 CC

7(revised) **III^{2}8 • C^{3}g (Doubled CC Inside, 0 in Denticles)** (?) I-3 R-3

Obverse III^{2}8– Top of 0 showing in denticles as raised curved bars in two adjacent denticle spaces below 0.

Reverse C^{3}g– Doubled large V CC mint mark. First C doubled strongly on lower left inside of loop. Second C tilted slightly to right and doubled slightly on lower inside of loop.

1890 O

26 **III^{2}14 • C^{3}a (890 Tops in Denticles)** (181) I-5 R-6

Obverse III^{2}14– Tops of 890 showing in denticles as shallow curved bar in denticle space below 8, raised curved bar in denticle space just to left of 9 and raised curved bar in denticle space just to left of 0.

28 **III^{2}16 • C^{3}a (Possible 0 Top in Denticles)** (181) I-2 R-5

Obverse III^{2}16– Thin curved bar in field at end of denticle space below 0 in date.

28A **III^{2}16 • C^{3}a (Possible 0 Top in Denticles, Clashed Obverse n & st)** (181) I-2 R-5

Obverse III^{2}16– Clashed die with faint partial incuse n of In from reverse next to Liberty head neck and partial st of Trust from reverse showing in right hair vee of lower hair edge.

1890 S

2(revised) **III^{2}9 • C^{3}b (S/S Left, 89 in Denticles)** (188) I-4 R-4

Obverse III^{2}9– Tops of 89 showing in denticles as raised curved bar in denticle space below 8 and shallow raised curved bar in field in denticle space below 9.

Reverse C^{3}b– IV S mint mark re-punched with original showing as broken arc in top middle of upper loop and a complete arc in middle of lower loop.

33 **III^{2}12 • C^{3}q (Possible 7 Top in Denticles, Possible S/S Lower Loop)** (181) I-2 R-5

Obverse III^{2}12– Possible middle top of 7 showing in denticle space between 90 as a slanted bar with lower right end. Date set much further right than normal.

Reverse C^{3}q– Possible IV S mint mark re-punched with filled top loop and horizontal bar in lower loop. Second high grade specimen need for confirmation.

1891 S

11 **III^{2}9 • C^{3}a (189 in Denticles)** (191) I-3 R-6

Obverse III^{2}9– Tops of 189 showing in denticles as raised bar in denticle space below 1, slightly raised curved bar in denticle space below and to left of 8, and faint curved diagonal bar in denticle space below 9.

1892 CC

10(revised)**III^{2}6 • C^{3}d (9 or 2 in Denticles, Wide CC)** (177) I-3 R-4

Obverse III^{2}6– Top of 9 or 2 showing in denticles has raised curved bar in field in denticle space between 9 and 2.

10A **III^{2}6 • C^{3}d (9 or 2 in Denticles, Wide CC, Clashed Obverse st)** (177) I-3 R-6

Obverse III^{2}6– Clashed die with faint partial incuse st of Trust from reverse showing in right hair vee of lower hair edge. Triple clashed die.

1892 O

12(revised) **III^{2}11 • C^{3}a (9 Below Hair, Overlapping Reeding)** (?) I-5 R-5

Obverse III^{2}11– Bottom of 9 showing just below hair to right of designers initial M as a raised curved bar that widens to the right.

Edge– Reeding on edge is overlapping for about 8 segments at three locations 3, 9 and 11 o'clock.

12A **III^{2}11 • C^{3}a (9 Below Hair, Overlapping Reeding, Clashed Obverse n)** (?) I-5 R-6

Obverse III^{2}11– Clashed die with faint partial incuse n of In from reverse showing next to Liberty head neck.

Edge– Reeding is overlapping for about 8 segments at three locations of 1, 5 & 11 o'clock. Collar has rotated CW 2 clock positions from un-clashed VAM 12.

1896 P

19 **III^{2}19 • C^{3}a (8 in Denticles)** <u>**TOP 100**</u> (190) I-5 R-5

Obverse III^{2}19– Top of 8 appears in two denticle spaces just below 8 as two raised and curved bars. Date slightly slanted with 1 closest to rim.

26 **III^{2}4 • C^{3}a (Possible 9 in Denticles)** (191) I-2 R-5

Obverse III^{2}4– Possible 9 top in denticles showing as raised curved bar well back in denticle space below 9, but not conclusive evidence.

1900 P

16(revised) **III^{2}23 • C^{4}/C^{3}b (2 Olive Reverse, 900 in Denticles)** <u>**HOT 50**</u> (189) I-5 R-3

Obverse III^{2}23– Tops of 900 showing in denticles as raised curved bars in single denticle space below 9, in two adjacent denticle spaces below first 0, and in single denticle space to left of second 0. Heavy die polishing lines in wheat leaves.

Reverse C^{4}/C^{3}b– Extra olive to right of olive connected to olive branch. Doubling at base of left olive leaf cluster, back of lower arrow head, right side of the eagle's nostril and eye, and upper feathers of eagle's left wing. Pitting about eagle's neck on some specimens.

19(revised) **III²28 • C⁴/C³d (2 Olive Reverse, 0 in Denticles)** **(189)** **I-2** **R-4**

Obverse III²28– Top of 0 shows in denticles as curved bar in denticle space between 00. Date in normal position.

Reverse C⁴/C³d– Extra olive to right of olive connected to olive branch. Doubling at base of left and lower olive leaf clusters, back of lower arrow head, and on right of two inner most right wing feathers next to leg.

1900 Proof

32 **III²27 • C³a (Near Date, 0 in Denticles)** **(?)** **I-3** **Proof**

Obverse III²27– Top of 0 shows in denticles as raised curved bar in denticle space between 00 and small curved tick in adjacent right denticle space. Date set further left than normal.

1900 O

46 **III²31 • C³a (Doubled First 0 Bottom, Near Date, Possible 0 in Denticles)** **(181)** **I-2** **R-5**

Obverse III²31– First 0 slightly doubled at bottom outside. Date set further left than normal. Possible 0 in denticles showing as raised curved bar in denticle space between 0's, but not conclusive evidence.

Reverse C³a– Very slight doubling at bottom of arrow heads. *Die marker*– Fine vertical die scratches at bottom outside of eagle's left leg and right side of eagle's left leg.

1901 O

15(revised) **III²12 • C⁴/C³d (2 Olive Reverse, 90 in Denticles)** **(181)** **I-3** **R-3**

Obverse III²12– Tops of 90 showing in denticles as raised curved bars in single denticle space below 9 and in single denticle space below 0.

Reverse C⁴/C³d– Extra olive to right of olive connected to olive branch. Doubling at base of top and bottom olive leaf cluster, back of lower arrow head and right of eagle's nostril. III O mint mark tilted left.

1903 S

6(revised) **III²3 • C⁴/C³c (903 in Denticles, 2 Olive Reverse)** **(189)** **I-4** **R-4**

Obverse III²3– Tops of 903 show in denticles as raised curved bars in single denticle space below 9, 0 & 3.

Reverse C⁴/C³c– Faint shallow extra olive to right of olive connected to olive branch. Doubling on edge of top leaf in lower olive leaf cluster, top edge of upper arrow feathers, back of lower arrow head, top feathers of eagle's left wing and right side of eagle's nostril and eye. V S mint mark set upright and slightly high.

BIBLIOGRAPHY

Breen, Walter, *Walter Breen's Complete Encyclopedia of U.S. and Colonial Coins*, Doubleday & F.C. I. Press, 1988.

Fey, Michael and Jeff Oxman, *The Top 100 Morgan Dollar Varieties: The VAM Keys,* 1996.

Flynn, Kevin, *A Collector's Guide to Misplaced Date*, 1997.

Flynn, Kevin, *Morgan Dollar Overdates, Over Mintmarks, Misplaced Dates and Clashed E Reverses,* 1998, Archive Press.

Oxman, Jeff, *SSDC Official Guide to the Hot 50 Morgan Dollar Varieties*, 2000.

Smith, A.M., *Visitors Guide to The U.S. Mint Philadelphia,* 1885.

Van Allen, Leroy C. and A. George Mallis, *Comprehensive Catalog & Encyclopedia of Morgan & Peace Dollars,* DLRC Press 3rd ed.1992, & 4th ed.1998 reprint.

Annual Report of the Director of the Mint to the Secretary of the Treasury for the Fiscal Year Ended June 30, 1896, U.S. Department of the Treasury, 1897, Manufacturer of Dies by Charles E. Barber, Engraver.

Annual Report of the Director of the Mint to the Secretary of the Treasury for the Fiscal Year Ended June 30, 1902, U.S. Department of the Treasury, 1903, Engraver's Department by Charles E. Barber, Engraver.

PHOTOGRAPHS OF MPDs

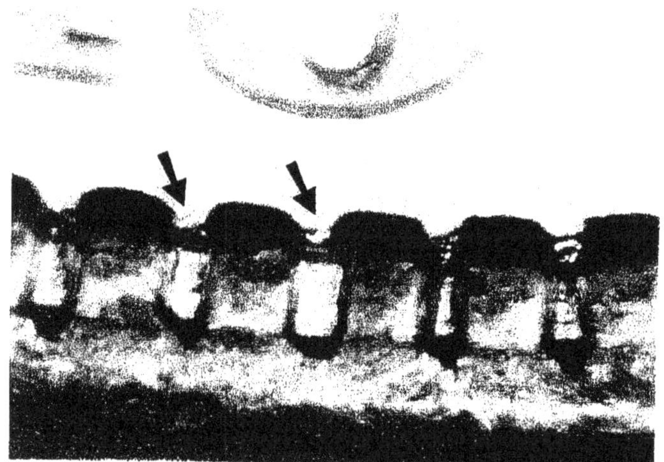
1879 S VAM 44 Possible 7 in Denticles

1880 P VAM 51 8 in Denticles

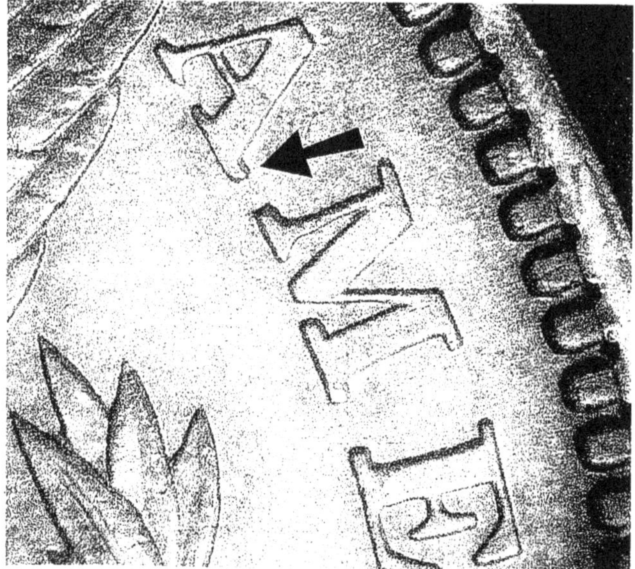
1880 P VAM 51 Doubled Legend

1880 P VAM 51 Doubled 880

1881 S VAM 52 8 in Denticles

1881 S VAM 53 8 in Denticles

1881 S VAM 61 Possible 1 in Denticles

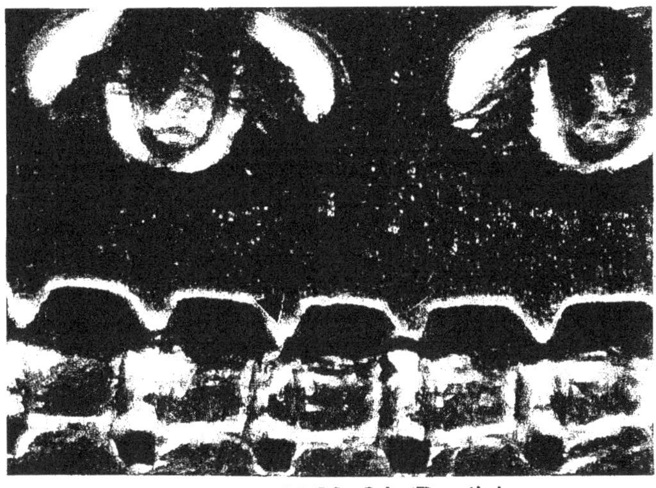
1882 P VAM 20 8 in Denticles

1882 P VAM 20 Doubled upper Reverse

1882 P VAM 23 8 in Denticles

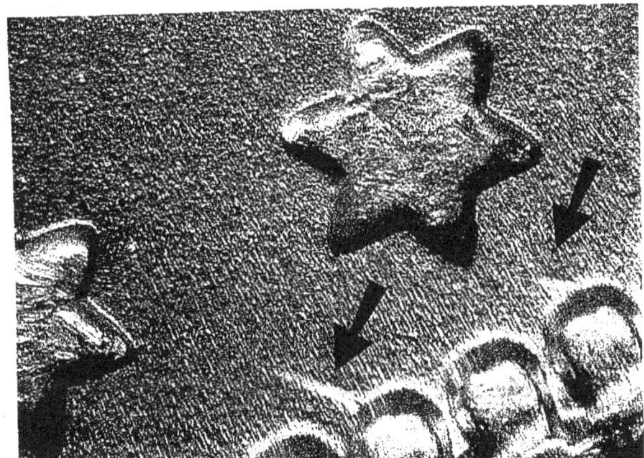
1882 P VAM 23 Die Gouges Second Rt. Star

1882 P VAM 24 Double 1 Base MPD

1882 P VAM 24 Doubled 882, Double MPD, Over Polished

1882 CC VAM 2 1 Top Below 8

1882 CC VAM 2 1 Top Below 8

1882 CC VAM 2 Polishing Lines Stars

1882 CC VAM 2 Polished Letters & Star

1882 CC VAM 2A Clashed n

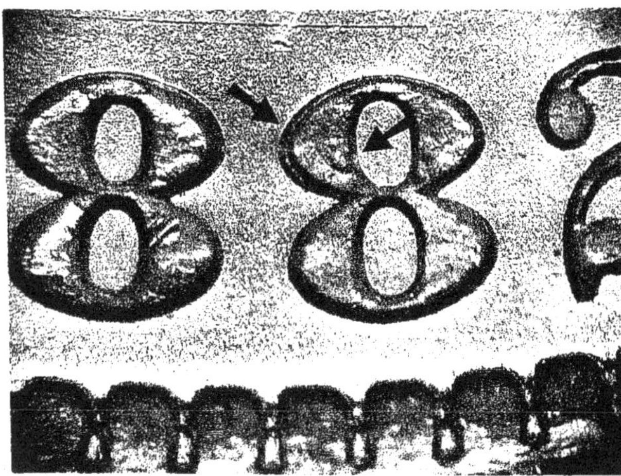

1882 CC VAM 2C Doubled 882, Die Chip 8

1882 CC VAM 2C Counterclash Lip

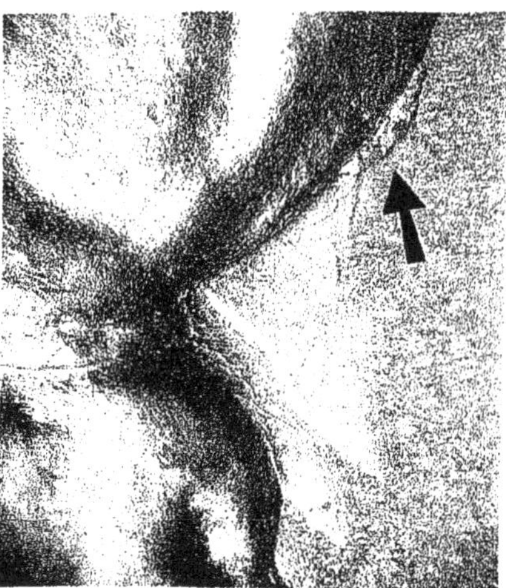

1882 CC VAM 2C Break Cap Back

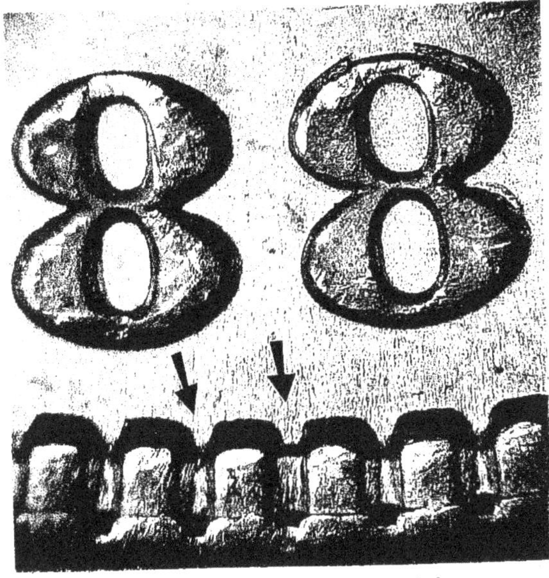

1883 P VAM 4 8 in Denticles

1883 P VAM 4 Doubled 1-83

1883 O VAM 39 Die Flakes First 8

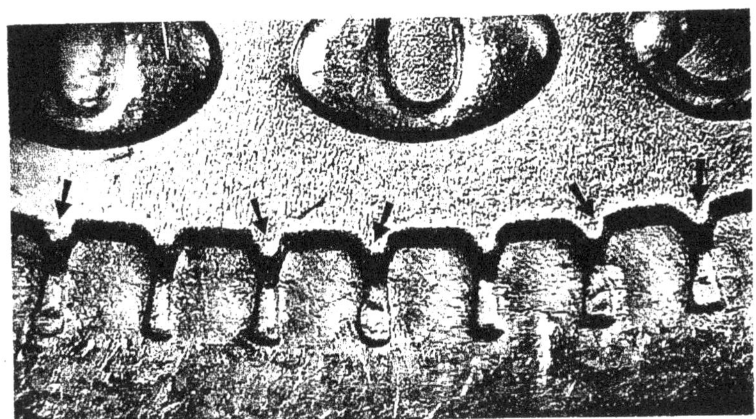

1883 O VAM 39 Date Digits in Denticles

1883 O VAM 40 1 in Denticles

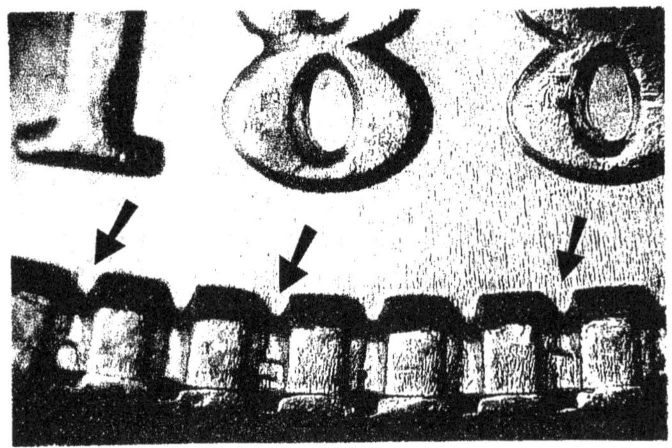

1884 P VAM 15 188 in Denticles

1884 P VAM 17 Possible 4 in Denticles

1884 P VAM 17 Die Scratches E

1884 P VAM 18 Possible 8 in Denticles

1884 O VAM 25 188 in Denticles

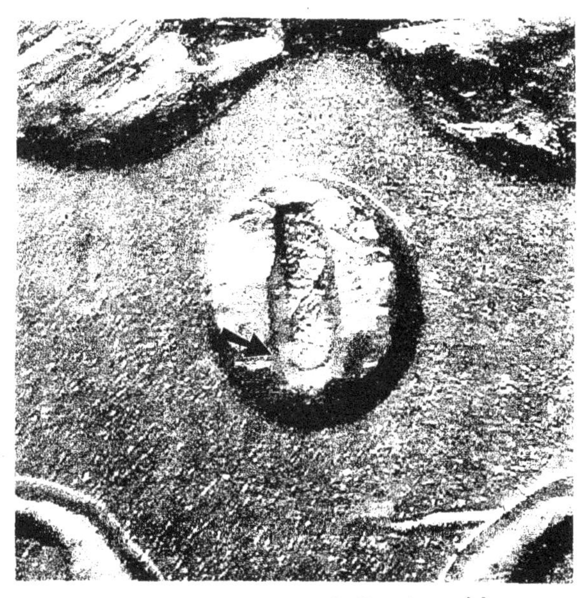

1884 O VAM 25 O/O Centered Low

1884 O VAM 37 18 in Denticles

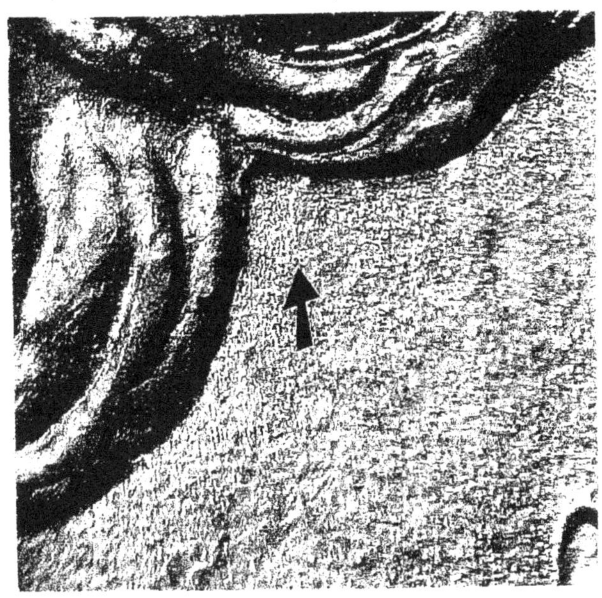

1884 O VAM 37A Clashed st

1884 O VAM 38 Possible 8 in Denticles

1884 O VAM 38
Doubled 1

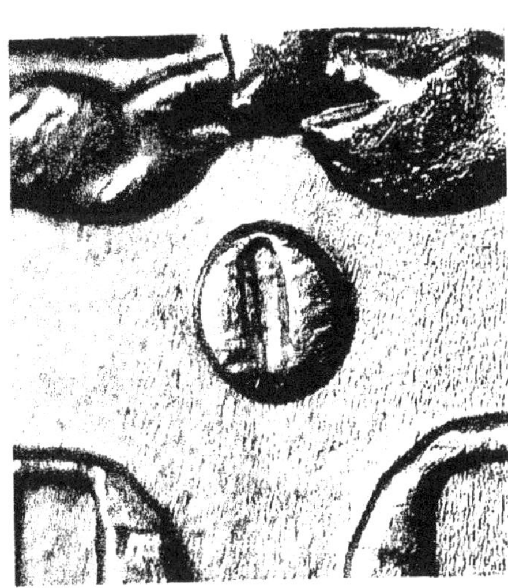

1884 O VAM 38 O Tilted Left

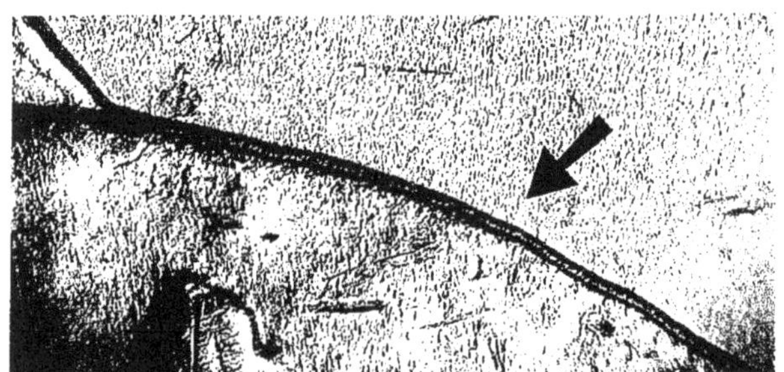

1884 O VAM 38 Doubled Phrygian Cap

1885 O VAM 17 8 in Denticles

1885 S VAM 8 885 in Denticles

1885 S VAM 9 S/S

1884 S VAM 8 18 in Denticles

1884 S VAM 9 884 in Denticles

1885 P VAM 28 Possible 8 in Denticles

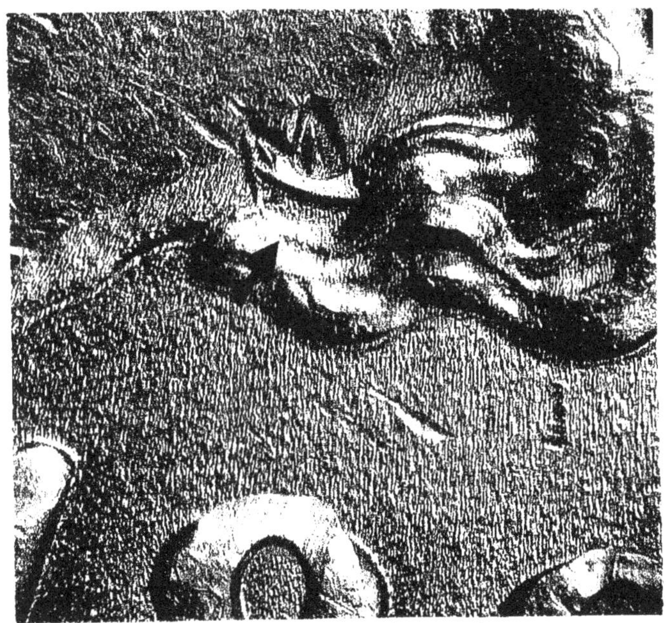

1886 P VAM 21 8 Below M

1886 P VAM 21 Doubled Reverse Lettering

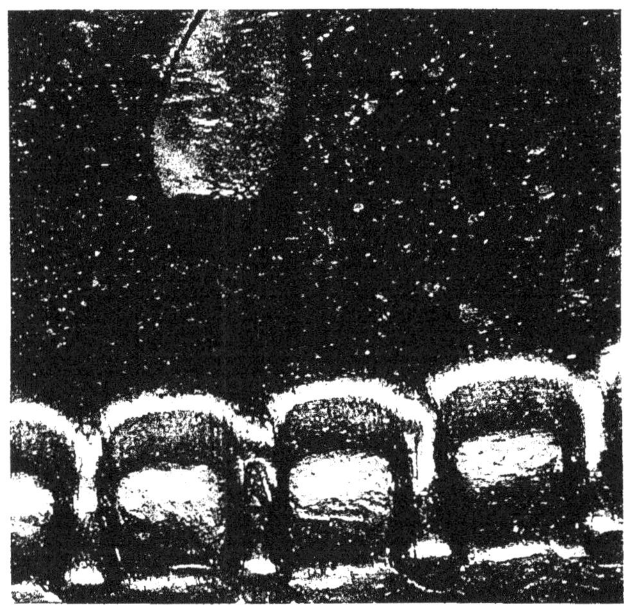

1887 P VAM 11 7 in Denticles

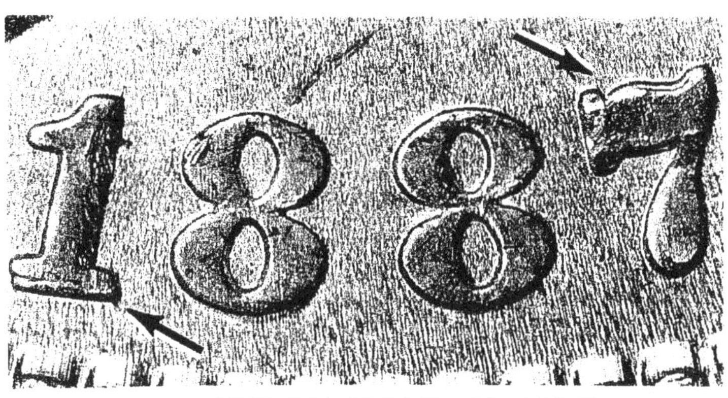

1887 P VAM 11 Doubled 18-7

1887 P VAM 13 Doubled Right Stars

1887 P VAM 13 7 in Denticles

1887 P VAM 13 Doubled AMERICA

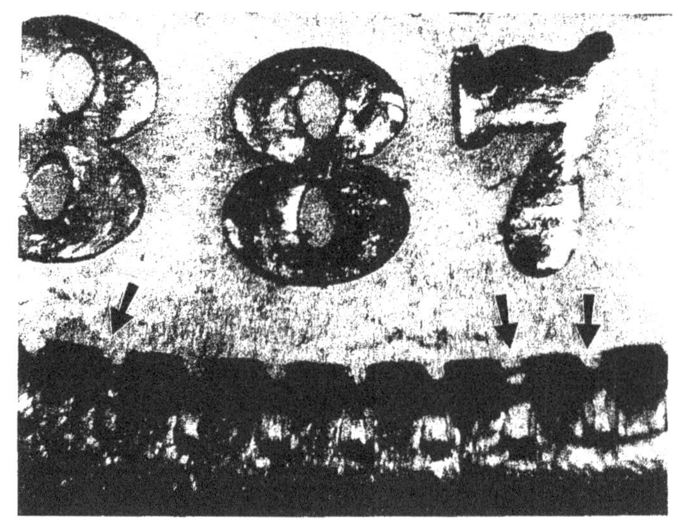

1887 P VAM 17 8-7 in Denticles

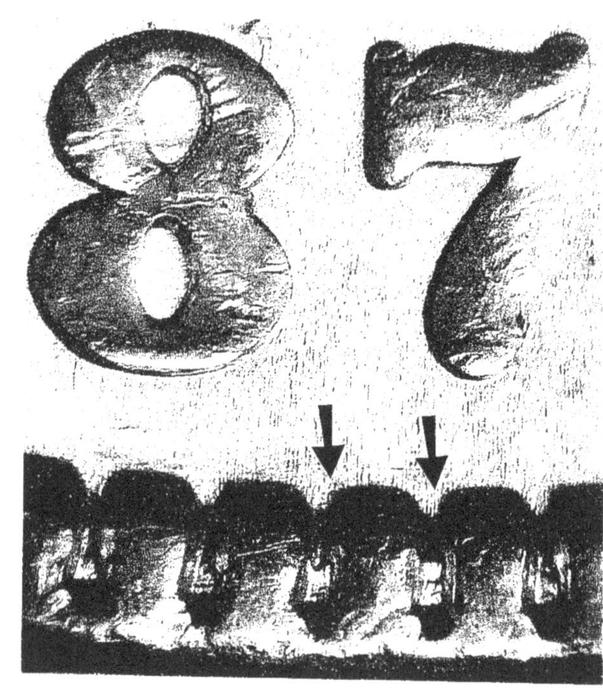

1887 P VAM 19 7 in Denticles

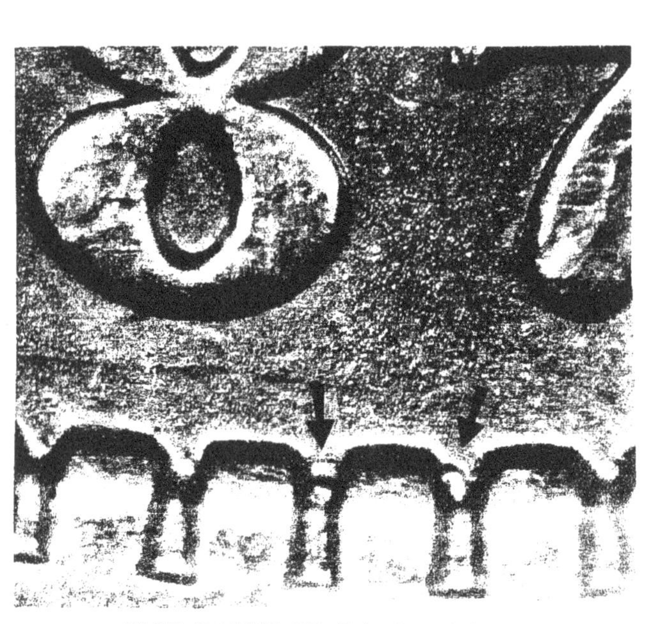

1887 O VAM 27 7 in Denticles

1887 O VAM 28 18-7 in Denticles

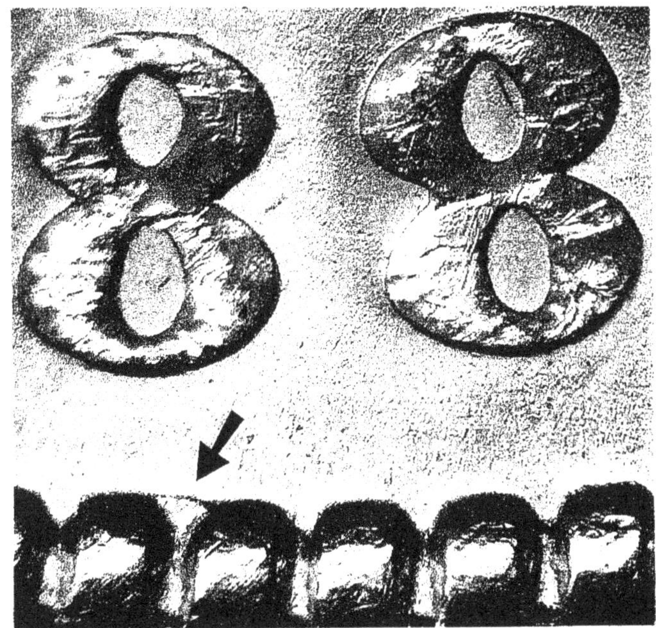

1888 P VAM 18 8 in Denticles

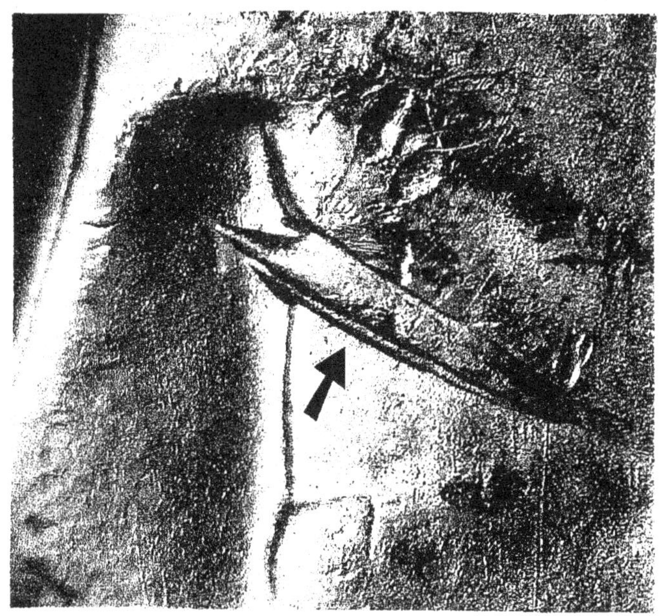

1888 P VAM 18 Doubled Eyelid

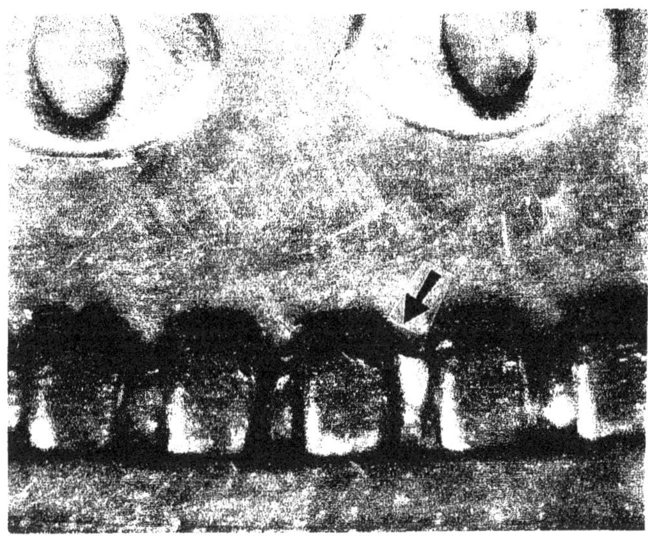

1888 Proof VAM 25 8 in Denticles

1888 Proof VAM 25 Doubled Date

1888 O VAM 6 Doubled 88, 8 in Denticles

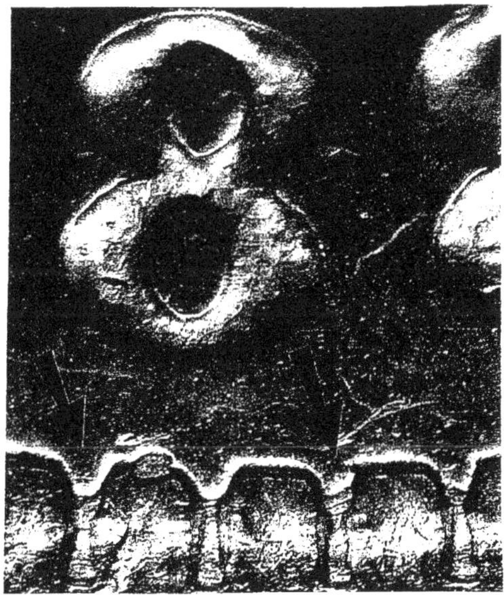

1888 O VAM 9 18-8 in Denticles

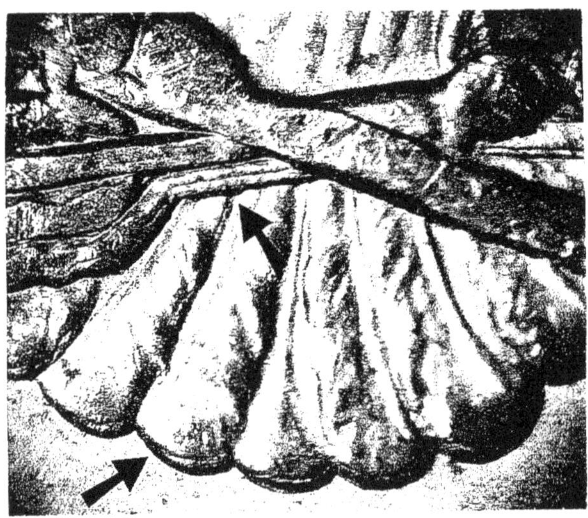
1888 O VAM 9 Doubled Arrows & Tail Feathers

1888 O VAM 9 Doubled Wreath

1888 O VAM 28 1 in Denticles

1888 O VAM 28 Doubled Ear

1888 O VAM 33 8 in Denticles

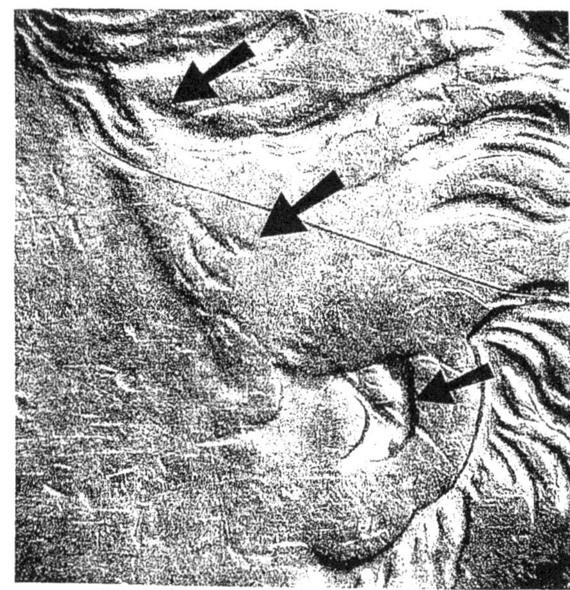
1888 O VAM 33 Die Gouge Hair to Ear

1889 P VAM 24 8 in Denticles

1890 P VAM 25 9 in Denticles

1890 P VAM 25A Clashed n

1890 P VAM 26 Possible 1 in Denticles

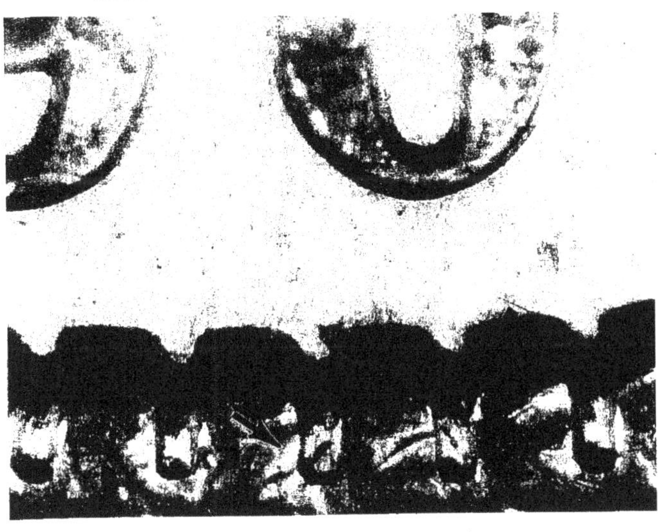
1890 CC VAM 7 0 in Denticles

1890 CC VAM 7 Doubled CC Inside

1890 O VAM 26 890 in Denticles

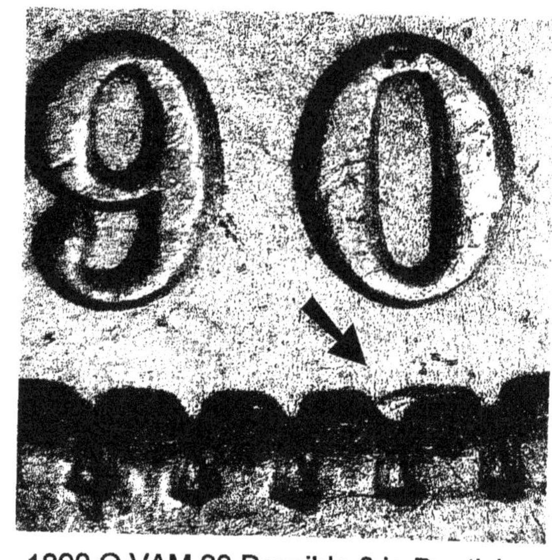

1890 O VAM 28 Possible 0 in Denticles

1890 O VAM 28A Clashed n

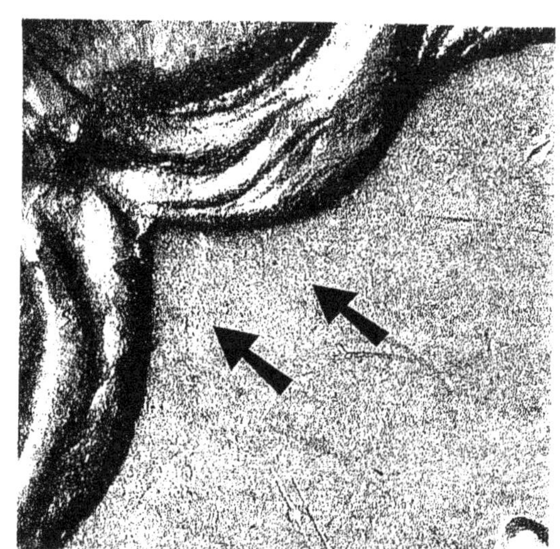

1890 O VAM 28A Clashed st

1890 S VAM 2 89 in Denticles

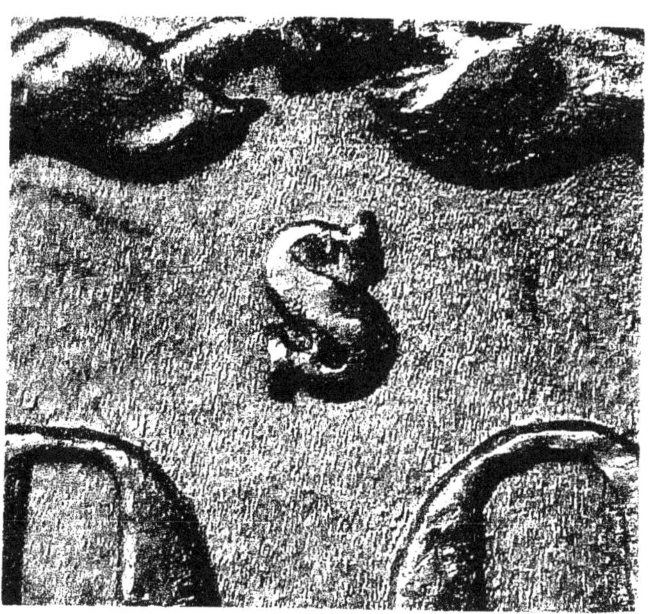

1890 S VAM 2 S/S Left

1890 S VAM 33 Possible 7 Top in Denticles

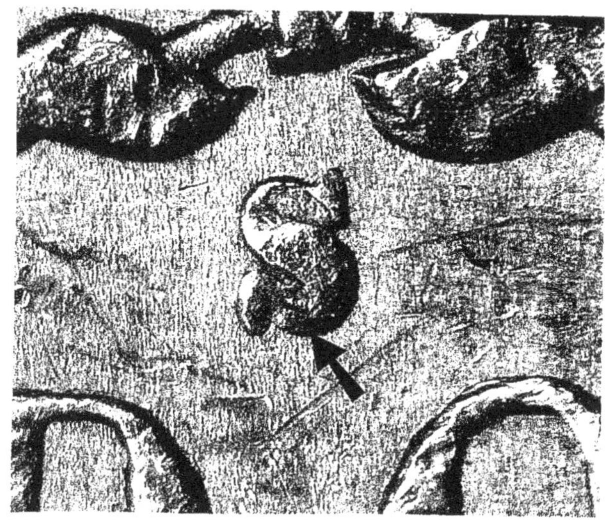

1890 S VAM 33 Possible S/S Lower Loop

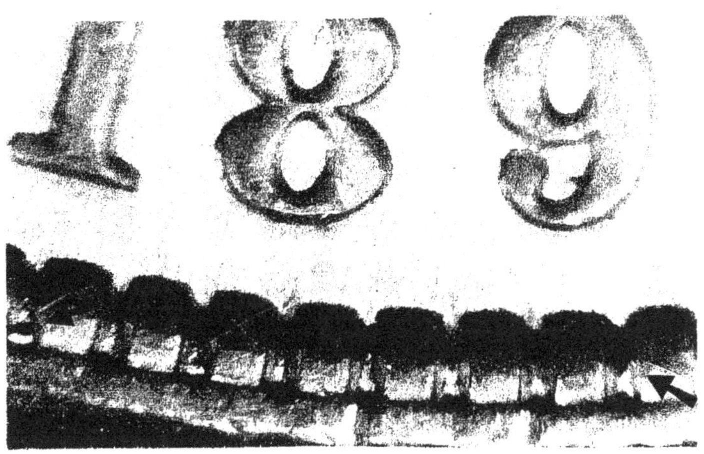

1891 S VAM 11 189 in Denticles

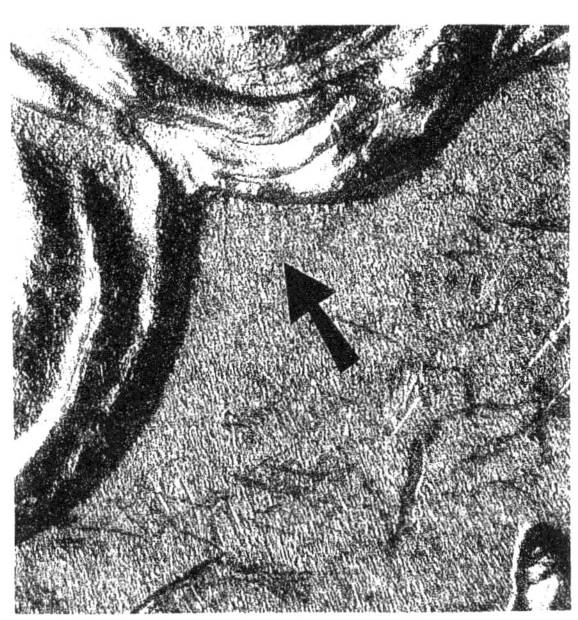

1892 CC VAM 10A Clashed st

1892 CC VAM 10 9 or 2 in Denticles

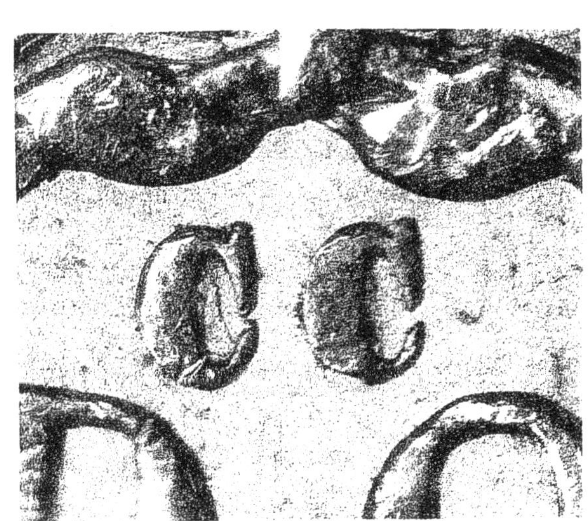

1892 CC VAM 10 Wide CC

1892 O VAM 12 9 Below Hair

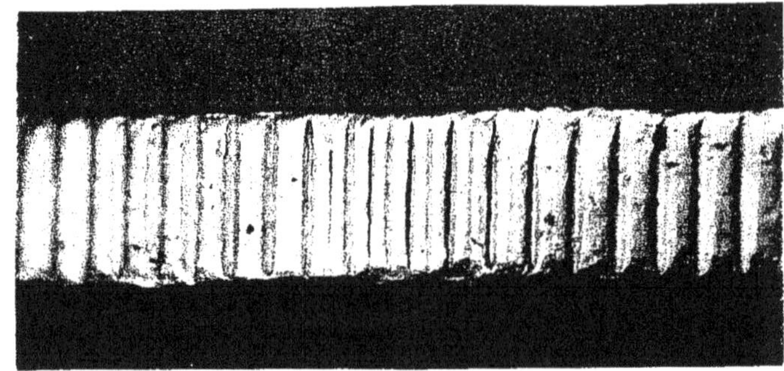

1892 O VAM 12 Overlapping Reeding 3 O'clock

1892 O VAM 12 Overlapping Reeding 9 O'clock

1892 O VAM 12 Overlapping Reeding 11 O'clock

1892 O VAM 12A Clashed n

1896 P VAM 19 8 in Denticles

1896 P VAM 26 Possible 9 in Denticles

1900 P VAM 16 Pitting Eagle's Neck

1900 P VAM 16 Polishing Lines Wheat Leaves

1900 P VAM 16 900 in Denticles

1900 P VAM 16 2 Olive Reverse

1900 P VAM 19 0 in Denticles

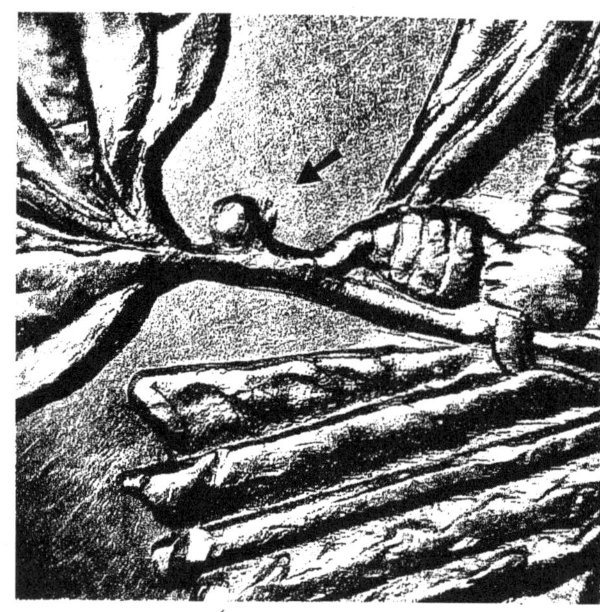

1900 P VAM 19 2 Olive Reverse

1900 Proof VAM 32 0 in Denticles

1900 O VAM 46 Doubled 0, Possible 0 in Denticles

1900 O VAM 46 Die Scratches Wing & Leg

1901 O VAM 15 90 in Denticles

1901 O VAM 15 2 Olive Reverse

1903 S VAM 6 903 in Denticles

1903 S VAM 6 2 Olive Reverse

FURTHER REFERENCES

Please check Amazon Kindle for Michael S. Fey, Ph.D., and Leroy Van Allen & A. George Mallis publications. For hard copy print of books, please contact Dr. Fey at RCI, P.O. Box C, Ironia, NJ 07845 or eMail: Feyms@aol.com.

Hard copy books are also available at *The Institute for Silver Dollar Education and Research*, at website: *Ilovesilver dollars.org* or by contacting Executive Director John Baumgart at John.Baumgart@comcast.net

Amazon Kindle

Fey, Michael S. 2019. *The Complete Virtual Guide to Pricing Your Morgan Silver Dollars*. 286 pp. RCI

Van Allen, Leroy, & A. George Mallis. 2023. *Part I or II or III of Three. Comprehensive Catalog and Encyclopedia or Morgan & Peace Dollars*. RCI Total 520 pp.

Leroy Van Allen. 2011. *Wonders of Morgan Dollars*. 139 pp. RCI

Leroy Van Allen. 2013. *Wonders of Peace Dollars*. 273 pp. RCI

Leroy Van Allen. 2006. *Morgan Dollars 8 & 7 Over 8 Tail Feather Story*. 52 pp. RCI

Leroy Van Allen. 2010. *1878 P 7 Tail Feather Morgan Dollar Attribution Guide*. 130 pp. RCI

Leroy Van Allen. 2006. *1878 S Morgan Dollar Attribution Guide*. 139 pp. RCI

Fey, Michael S. 2009 The Top 100 Morgan Dollar Varieties: The VAM Keys

FURTHER REFERENCES

Hard Copy Books

Fey, Michael S. 2019. The Top 100 Morgan Dollar Varieties: The VAM Keys. 286 pp. RCI

Fey, Michael S. 2008. *A Decade of Top 100 Insights*. RCI 174 pp.

Van Allen, Leroy. 1991. *RotaFlip Die Rotation Booklet and Guide*. 1991. RCI

Kimpton, M.D., Mark. 2005. *Elite Clashed Morgan Dollars*. RCI 160 pp

Van Allen, Leroy, & A. George Mallis. 2023. *Comprehensive Catalog and Encyclopedia or Morgan & Peace Dollars*. RCI Total 520 pp.

Van Allen, Leroy 2011. *Wonders of Morgan Dollars*. 139 pp. RCI

Van Allen, Leroy 2013. *Wonders of Peace Dollars*. 273 pp. RCI

Van Allen, Leroy 2006. *Morgan Dollars 8 & 7 Over 8 Tail Feather Story*. 52 pp. RCI

Van Allen, Leroy 2010. *1878 P 7 Tail Feather Morgan Dollar Attribution Guide*. 130 pp. RCI

Van Allen, Leroy 2006. *1878 S Morgan Dollar Attribution Guide*. 139 pp. RCI

Van Allen, Leroy 2013. *Die Gouges and Scratches Peace Dollar Attribution Guide. 109 pp* RCI

Van Allen, Leroy 2008. *1921 Scribbles Morgan Dollar Attribution Guide*. 234 pp. RCI

Van Allen, Leroy. 2013. *Misplaced Date Digits Morgan Dollar Attribution Guide*. 57 pp RCI

Van Allen, Leroy. 2017. *Dashed Under 8 Morgan Dollar Attribution Guide*. 53 pp. RCI

Van Allen, Leroy. 2009. *Overdates and Over Mint Marks of Morgan Dollar Attribution Guide*. 53 pp. RCI

Van Allen, Leroy. 2015. *Denticle & Die Impressions Morgan Dollar Attribution Guide*. 109 pp. RCI

Van Allen, Leroy. 2009. *1921 P Infrequently Reeded or Wide Reeding Morgan Dollar Attribution Guide*. 31 pp. RCI

Van Allen, Leroy. 2011 *Amazing Changing 1921 S VAM 1B Thorn Head Morgan Dollar*. 2011. 22 pp. RCI

Van Allen, Leroy. 2009. *1889 P Doubled Ear Morgan Dollar Attribution Guide*. 32 pp. RCI

Van Allen, Leroy. 2016. *Micro o and Other Counterfeit Morgan and Peace Dollars*. 191 pp RCI

Van Allen, Leroy. 2005. *Micro o Mint Mark on Morgan Dollars*. 32 pp. RCI

Van Allen, Leroy. 2005. *Die Markers for 1921 Morgan and Peace Proof Dollars*. 9 pp. RCI

Van Allen, Leroy and Baumgart, John. 1992-Date Various VAM Book Yearly Supplements. RCI

www.ingramcontent.com/pod-product-compliance
Ingram Content Group UK Ltd.
Pitfield, Milton Keynes, MK11 3LW, UK
UKHW062000290726
14090UKWH00021B/1307

9 798991 964852